Mastering
MONOLOGUES
and Acting Sides

HOW TO AUDITION
SUCCESSFULLY
FOR BOTH TRADITIONAL
AND NEW MEDIA

Janet Wilcox

ALLWORTH PRESS
NEW YORK

Allworth Press books may be purchased in bulk at special discounts for
sales promotion, corporate gifts, fund-raising, or educational purposes.
Special editions can also be created to specifications. For details, contact the
Special Sales Department, Allworth Press, 307 West 36th Street, 11th Floor,
New York, NY 10018 or info@skyhorsepublishing.com.

15 14 13 12 11   5 4 3 2 1

Published by Allworth Press
An imprint of Skyhorse Publishing
307 West 36th Street, 11th Floor, New York, NY 10018.

Allworth Press® is a registered trademark of Skyhorse Publishing, Inc.®,
a Delaware corporation.

www.allworth.com

Library of Congress Cataloging-in-Publication Data
Wilcox, Janet.
   Mastering monologues and acting sides : how to audition successfully
for both traditional and new media / Janet Wilcox.
      p. cm.
   Includes index.
   ISBN 978-1-58115-866-3
   1. Acting—Auditions. 2. Monologue.   I. Title.
   PN2071.A92W55 2011
   792.02'8—dc23
                                        2011022647
Printed in the United States of America

Contents

John Brosnan • Introduction to *The Mile-High Club* Written by
Rosanne Welch • Scene One Considerations for *The Mile-High
Club* • Some Evident Clues for Scene Two of *The Mile-High Club*
• Overview for *The Mile-High Club* Scene Three • Overview for
Nurses Who Kill . . . Written by Ann Noble and Created by Ann
Noble and Chane't Johnson • Overview for *Smudge* Written by
Rachel Axler • Scene Considerations for *Smudge*

Preface

At the heart of most Academy Award®-winning performances is a great monologue. Tony® winners take plays to new heights with a soliloquy at the core of their work, and Emmy® winners fill the screen with memorable solo scenes. It is no wonder that novice actors aspire to do a monologue with gusto straight from the gate.

When an actor first decides to take the acting craft seriously, he will begin the climb up monologue mount. Like so many actors, he will struggle to make a solitary performance seem real and dynamic. This element of acting is a rite of passage in class work, and a defining moment in great plays and movies. Classic Academy Award®-winning monologues often send chills down your spine. The featured soliloquy is a perfect fit for the performer and often a tour de force of the actor's career. For example, Virginia Madsen's speech in *Sideways* was a memorable highlight of her Oscar®-nominated performance.

Award-winning performances aside, writers will always take advantage of the powerful impact that soliloquies deliver in a script. Who can forget *Ferris Bueller's Day Off*, a *Law & Order* murder confession, or a frank soliloquy from *The Office*? Woody Allen even showcased Larry David's comedic talents with long monologues in his movie *Whatever Works*. The truth is, monologues appear in scripts throughout an actor's career. They are used in commercials, TV programs, and films. A monologue isn't just for a theater audition; it's woven into everything from webisodes to staged testimonials. It's also the litmus test for many actors reaching for a higher level of performance. An inexperienced actor may be asked to perform one by an agent or casting director to demonstrate competence for any number of reasons.

Of course, monologues may be used to showcase skills and to give industry gatekeepers a chance to evaluate an actor's talent, but the soliloquy can also help an actor keep fit for any job. Everything a performer does to prepare for a monologue will yield results when he is asked to do a last-minute audition or quickly learn a rewrite on the set. Like scales for a singer, it keeps the actor ready to hit the highs and lows and smooth out the breaks if practiced properly.

PRACTICE MAKES YOU A PRO

This book attempts to encourage actors to embrace a good work ethic to stay in shape between performances and thus to be ready to seize any opportunities that may arise. Scripts are presented for practice and classroom performances. There are also plenty of resources listed to explore additional monologues and audition scenes, including those at your fingertips on the Internet.

These Web references are only suggestions for you to begin your search for material. Sites can always change, so use key words to find new resources. There is no limit to what you can discover, so keep digging. My list is a jumping-off place for you to begin your continuous exploration of what the Web has to offer.

I wrote this book primarily because I realized that the monologue is a benchmark throughout an actor's career. First, it's an elusive challenge. Then, it's a comfortable conversation, and finally, it can be a powerful showpiece for any actor. The search for new material never ends, because an actor evolves, grows, ages, and becomes hungrier to do more challenging parts.

When I began my acting classes, I didn't really like to work on monologues as stand-alone speeches and always preferred doing scenes with other actors. This is ironic because many of my voice-over auditions and bookings are monologues. A voice-over artist performs solo scenes for commercials, narrations, animated characters, audio books, and video games. Therefore, I am constantly trying to imagine that I am in a scene with someone who is not present. This takes a lot of imagination and creativity. In addition, I teach a range of students and witness the many obstacles new and seasoned actors alike consistently face in creating credible performances.

I have also had the opportunity to revisit rudimentary acting classes at UCLA Extension, where I also teach a voice-over class, and I realized that many students begin to work on monologues before first acquiring a strong performing arts foundation. I wanted, therefore, to address the one challenging constant in an actor's career: the monologue. I also will compare the soliloquy performance to auditions in which an actor only has an isolated portion of a script, or the "sides." These may be used for cold reads if the actor has little preparation time.

The monologue and sides are often removed from a full-length script, and the performer must fill in the missing details. In either case, an actor must rely on his imagination to embellish a partial script and make choices that are appropriate to the role and to the screenwriter's vision. These performances require the actor to envision a scene partner and a setting even if a casting director reads the cue lines when sides are used for an audition. Auditioning with sides has a partial interactive element that is missing with a monologue because someone reads the other character's lines, but the quality of the scene partner can be hit or miss. In addition, the common problems of nerves and doubt can derail an audition with sides in the same way that nagging negatives can rob an actor of the ability to perform a monologue well. This book focuses on strategies to help you analyze the type of isolated scenes and monologues that you will have to do for classes, auditions, and jobs.

It is important, however, to note that you must always read a whole script or play if you have it for an audition scene. If you don't, a casting director or teacher will know you didn't do all of your homework. Also, you should be reading full plays and scripts on a regular basis to fully understand how scenes and soliloquies evolve from larger scenarios. The library and Internet are great resources for scripts and plays. By analyzing how scenes and monologues emerge from whole scripts, you'll be better prepared to perform auditions, even if you only have a small section of a script.

YOU MUST ALWAYS STUDY

Whether you're in classes, doing a student film, performing theater, or being paid to act, you must continue to fine-tune your acting skills. This does not always mean that you have to spend money. It takes a great deal of discipline to succeed as an actor. You must have the determination to keep doing monologues and scenes whether you're broke, famous, or fumbling in your career.

Studies can be of life, plays, or under the tutelage of a great director. It is naïve to think that this process ever ends. On the other hand, it's exciting to know that there are infinite skills to master and fascinating real life-stories to explore.

Those life stories can be told in on-camera commercials, soap operas, films, television episodes, plays, short films, webisodes, and even in voice acting. There is work in all of these areas if a performer can adapt to the styles of each, whether it is a traditional acting style or a more improvisation-driven technique required for a webisode. An actor is a living, breathing, embodiment of life's travails and triumphs. Writers and directors channel their artistic visions through thespians. Pursing an acting career can also be enjoyable if you keep a good survival job and have an adventurous spirit.

I used a game model in my book *Voiceovers: Techniques and Tactics for Success* to keep an actor on target. I believe that the challenge and joy of creating a riveting monologue performance or compelling scene is enough of a carrot to keep you striving for more. After all, what's more fun than being at the center of attention with a good story? You can be a healer, spoiler, and sage all at once. It's a powerful feeling. So savor the joy of the journey and begin to learn a few tricks of the trade to guide you along the way. I've included interviews with industry experts to explore the practical applications of these techniques.

This book, like my voice-over book, is based on an online model and will point you to ways you can enrich your work on your own. You'll be able to pick and choose resources that are appropriate to your specific needs and interests. You can always study with me too. Just go to www.janetwilcox.com for details.

The beginning chapters present acting techniques and exercises. Basic ideas are covered first, and then more advanced concepts are introduced. There is a range of exercises to encourage you to strengthen traditional acting skills and expand your improvisation techniques to stay fluid and flexible for new challenges. Many new media productions may require good impromptu acting due to tight budgets; plus directors often ask you to make choices quickly on the spot in auditions.

As audiences have embraced reality TV and YouTube, a more authentic realism in acting has emerged, so it is important to include uncensored improvisation exercises in your acting workouts. You'll find plenty of media examples and Web references to explore different performing styles. Industry experts discuss what is expected of professional actors doing auditions and performances in different settings. Practice scripts allow you to play with different characters as needed. You can turn to the appendix for all of the resources and checklists. The CD offers tips from professionals who have worked in a range of performance environments as well.

Just remember not to take yourself too seriously. Shed the trappings of your ego and inner fears, and allow yourself to perform freely with all the exercises that follow.

So turn the page and begin to make sense of monologue madness and audition sides that can lead to acting jobs in traditional and new media arenas.

Acknowledgments

A wonderfully talented group of generous creative people made this book possible. Many contributors gave their time for interviews or they shared samples of their writing. I am so grateful to everyone who helped me bring this book to you.

I especially want to thank Tad Crawford, Bob Porter, Claire Abramowitz, Cindy Peng, and the staff at Allworth Press and Skyhorse Publishing for guiding me through this process. There were so many talented readers and editors who helped along the way, but Sue O'Neal deserves special recognition for her insightful comments at all stages of this undertaking. Lindsay Bajo should also be recognized for her considerable expertise throughout the whole process.

In addition, I express my heartfelt gratitude to the following people and organizations: Simon Anthony Abou-Fadel, Richard Armida, Rachel Axler, Joan Baker, Shari Becker, Ray Bengston, Bob Bergen, Geoffrey Bird, Allen Blumberg, John Brosnan, Jill Burrichter, Craig Campobasso, Lea Carey, Jake Carpenter, Christina Chan, Cameron Cressman, Kaitlan Cressman, Sunda Croonquist, Godfrey Danchimah, Laura Danilov, Michelle Danner, Edge Studio, Jill Edwards, Riley Ellis, Alberto Ferreras, Lee Garlington, William Germano, Brian Gramo, Rob Granlund, Sean Gulian, Sara Guttman, HBO, Mathew Harrison, Blair Hickey, Elizabeth Hiles, Harlan Hogan, Susan Bullington Katz, Kristen Kay, Kristof Konrad, Michael Kostroff, Chelsea Lail, Diane Lake, Eugene Lazarev, Dan Leslie, Carl Lindahl, Bob Luke, Bonnie MacBird, Shanley McDonald, John Matthew, Michael Maxwell, Evangeline Morphos, Ann Noble,

Tim Nolan, Lucas K. Peterson, Michael Presky, Talmadge Ragan, Allison Reeds, Bradley Retzloff, Josefa Salinas, Beverly Sanders, Paul Sills, Caroline Sinclair, Selena Smith, Mike Soliday, Chris Spencer, Spotlight PR Company, Micaela Stepanovich, Troy Stone, Mark Subias, Stephanie Thomas, John Truby, Douglas E. Welch, Rosanne Welch, Pat Whiteman, Colleen Wilcox, Kathryn Willingham, Stewart F. Wilson-Turner, Sue Winik, James Yukich, Michael Yurchak, and Mark Zimmerman.

Above all, I am very grateful for Chane't Johnson's contribution to the book. Sadly she has passed on, but her webisode contribution remains to be a wonderful example for actors to study.

I am appreciative of anyone and everyone who inspired me to explore acting. My husband Paul and son Peter deserve extra recognition for their patience and support. I am also grateful to my brothers Garry, David, and Dennis for giving me so much to aspire to in life. Above all, I'm thankful for having such wonderful parents who taught me so much about courage, honesty, and humor.

1

Connecting to the Craft and Your Acting Partner

A monologue is, in a way, a misnomer although it is a single speech delivered by a sole actor. It should be called an *omnilogue* or *überlogue*, because it is all encompassing for a character. Many life-altering moments in a character's life are crystallized in the short performance. A cast of characters plays a role in shaping this one speech. Mothers, fathers, friends, and enemies along the way influence this speech.

An actor faces many challenges with a monologue. It can be a nerve-wracking experience to perform this acting showpiece in a class or on auditions, especially for the novice actor. Sometimes, the soliloquy is dramatically intense and requires a gamut of emotions in a short time span. Often, an actor has only a few minutes to convey the character's very essence.

The writer may rely on the monologue to solidify a theme or resolve a dramatic conflict. The actor must deliver this portion of the story with the intensity that it deserves. This is no easy feat for a novice actor especially: all at once the performer must summon a range of emotions, learn lines, and build a backstory for an isolated scene.

It makes little sense to begin with a task that requires such strong acting techniques. It makes even less sense to perform an isolated part of a script without first understanding how it evolves from a complete story line. Inexperienced actors are often asked to perform a monologue; yet they may not have the time to read a play or film script first. Frequently it's easier to pick out a soliloquy from a compilation book, partly because the actor doesn't know where to start. So the novice will select a script that *feels* right.

I've created this handbook to help make sense of the *stand-alone* monologues actors may perform in a range of situations. I also explore the isolated scenes, or *sides,* that are used for auditions. This book is no substitute for the proper study of acting, and any serious performer must pursue every opportunity to work with a qualified teacher and practice the craft in a range of performance arenas. An actor can, however, use this guide for a course of study before taking a class or performing an important audition. A seasoned professional can also utilize the streamlined techniques and practical industry advice to help prepare for hectic last-minute auditions.

Think of this manual as a home study course that will assist you if you can't benefit from a qualified coach or perform a whole play. It's also a workbook to keep you ready for auditions between jobs. Acting is active, so you will be asked to perform exercises and break down monologues. Many exercises explore your own life, so you can personalize your work and examine realistic scenarios. You can also use what you learn to help you employ the *as if* idea in acting if you can't quite relate to an experience in a script. In other words, you'll substitute something in your own life to connect to something that your character is experiencing. If, for example, I'm playing a character who is a drug addict, then I have to find something in my life that makes me addictive. Perhaps I drink too much coffee. I can use this idea as I think about playing a drug addict.

I was very lucky to have studied with wonderful acting teachers through the years. I've benefited from all of the insights and methods I've learned from these instructors. I owe so much of my everyday acting tools to the generous teachers who have shared insights into so many traditional acting techniques. To fully understand these approaches to acting, you need to study with a qualified teacher and take the time to absorb these processes.

In this book, I'm attempting to create a very simple easy guide for busy actors and will not dwell on the diverse methods that I have studied. You can consult in-depth classes and books for specific traditional acting techniques as you progress in your career.

In fact, I strongly encourage you to study every method that inspires you to perfect your acting to the highest levels. Draw on the strong internal connections and sense memory techniques of Lee Strasberg. Open yourself to the interactive work encouraged by Sanford Meisner. Get playful and use your imagination with the theater games of Viola Spolin and Paul Sills. Expand your voice and body with the Alexander technique. Study classical movement and stage combat. Investigate the well-defined systems of Stanislavski that explore events and conflicts that characters encounter.

I am indeed indebted to every teacher I ever studied with and owe so much of my technique to them. You, too, will find a greater understanding of your craft as you learn unique acting methods. For this book, however, I've attempted to create something that is fun, straightforward, and easy to grasp for the active actor who is trying to create inspired monologues and scenes for a variety of performances and auditions.

Always remember to be relaxed and focused as you play around with different roles. Creativity flows best when you are unrestricted. Tension in the body and mind will only stop you from reaching your goal to perform your scripts effectively.

So begin to demystify your monologue and audition scene performances and enjoy the process!

BEING LOST

Nothing can be worse than being lost. Most people feel isolated and vulnerable. Inexperienced actors can feel this way when they perform a first monologue or scene. Pressure mounts even before the words are spoken, partly because the stakes are high. The actor may be facing a first acting class or a chance to do an audition for a part. Whatever the situation, an actor usually makes matters worse by concentrating on the wrong things.

However, if the performer just focuses on what the character needs, he will probably forget about his nerves. After all, there is usually a lot at stake. The monologue or scene may revolve around a crisis or problem that needs to be solved. The character may confront a troubling situation or have a major revelation.

The performer is pulling so much together in a soliloquy; the scene may convey a moral code or relieve a dramatic conflict. A monologue may challenge an audience or imagined scene partner with uncomfortable ideas. Deep dark secrets from the past can be revealed to help the character move on to the next step in his life. The scenario can point to defeat and uncertain demise. It can also release tension and bring joy. In short, it is anything but boring, dull, or passive. A monologue or audition scene conveys a profound moment in a play or script. It makes perfect sense if an actor understands how this small scene fits into a larger dramatic story. Sometimes we must lose focus to gain clarity, and I believe this can be helpful to an actor who is tackling a monologue or scene for the first time. So be ready to let go of your fears of doing something less than perfect as you rehearse.

Failure is a part of learning and it also is a big part of success. Art has no easy answers. In fact, it is the imperfections that we all share that often draw us to one another. A writer often uses an opposing character to expose these flaws and help us understand our lives in difficult situations. So begin now and lose yourself. Let go of your ego and drive to succeed.

DO YOU TANGO?

Dancing with a partner is a lot like acting with a partner; someone leads and someone follows. If you're not careful, you can step on a toe or your companion will trample on your feet. Nonetheless, if you're lucky, your movements will flow almost as if they are connected. It will be like singing a duet with another singer in perfect harmony. Acting with a partner is at its best when two people unite and interact freely.

It often may be a relief to audition for parts with a partner or even a casting director reading the lines—some of the pressure is off you to carry the lead. However, don't be fooled by having a fellow actor lead the way to stimulate your responses.

Whether you are performing a monologue or auditioning with an isolated scene, you still need to know what your immediate needs and wants are. In both scenarios, you'll have to know what you are fighting for and what your objective is. You'll express your desires out loud and expect some kind of feedback.

If you are doing a monologue, you'll have to imagine how your partner reacts. If you perform a scene, you'll either react to a reader or a fellow actor's performance. Your cue line can be flat and passionless, so you still have to know what you want and what you need from your partner.

In both instances, you'll need to analyze your scene and your partner's objectives. If you are performing a scene, you need to be familiar with your fellow actor's lines as cues so you know when to speak your next line. You'll also want to determine what is important to your opposing character and how you may be an obstacle to her desires.

In some cases, when we have a scene partner, we may feel off the hook because we can react to someone else's work. We may even be tempted to rehearse in a planned fashion so that we recite our dialogue the same way no matter how our fellow actor delivers a line. In either instance, we may be using the words as a crutch and not preparing a scene as well as we should.

Above all, you want to stay fluid and ready to go with whatever happens in real time. Steve Martin discussed this idea on *The Today Show* when he talked about his experience acting with Meryl Streep and Alec Baldwin on the movie *It's Complicated*. He said doing a scene with these performers is like playing tennis, because you never know where the ball is going to land. It's great to draw on this example when thinking about your own work. You don't want to plan every detail and be stiff. Try to remember to relax and forget your rehearsal. Use your imaginary world to stimulate new thoughts. Really listen and react to your fellow performer. Life just happens, and that is what you should try to replicate when you act. You should react freely to the ups and downs and unexpected turns in every scene.

Like dancers, actors can be dancing different steps or be in unison in a scene. Think of the game of tug-of-war. Sometimes we pull because we are stronger or our partner pulls because we have a weak moment. The drama builds in a situation as someone gains ground. An actor enhances this dynamic by having a thorough understanding of the desires and conflicts that each character faces. This is the essence of scene work.

Observe Authentic Acting Scenes

Since sides are used in auditions, you need to observe all sorts of interactions in real life. There are so many great scenes unfolding at the coffee shop, office, and shopping mall. A customer may go ballistic with a sales clerk. Can you figure out what's really going on? Make some choices; look to see the bigger picture and consider the underlying causes. Is it possible that a lover just dumped this person? Start to study interactions everywhere you go.

Do the same for short scenes in movies and TV shows. Record segments and review them after you've had a chance to list each of the character's needs, wants, and motivations. Compare real-life scenes with TV and film scenarios. Start to notice what seems phony or authentic. It's all about going beneath the words and replicating believable behaviors.

I can say, "Please pass the salt," with one hundred different thoughts underneath the line. For example, I can be thinking, "My toe hurts," or "I hate you," or "Should I have dessert?" The options are endless. You have to play with choices and make ones that are consistent with what you and your opposing character are trying to get out of life at a particular time.

Sometimes we want to be left alone. We don't want people intruding into our lives. There are other times we need companionship desperately. The response of our partner may or may not change our behavior. If we have crossed a line and done something unforgivable, then we may never connect.

Random meetings can create a spark between two people who share a desire. Perhaps two people meet at the doorstep of an apartment they both want to rent. In this case, the interaction will be intense and competitive. If there is a romantic undertone, then underhandedness may give way to love.

Think about your day. When are you open to others? When are you reaching out to be heard? What are the specific things you're wanting? How is this different if you are with a close friend or a stranger? On the other hand, in what instances do you shut people out of your life? When do you ignore people? What chain of events created your need for isolation?

Consider the silent impressions that you have about the other person. They're like thought balloons. You always have your own internal dialogue that is hidden. Use that when you work on a scene. Think about what your secret ruminations are as you hear your partner's words. In fact, come up with a whole improvised inner monologue about your scene partner that expresses your unexpressed thoughts. Add this underlying dialogue to your scene work.

Understand Group Dynamics

Analyze monologues or scenes you have with your friends and family. When do you lead the way, and when do you follow? Who do you make laugh, and who makes you laugh? What groups bring out the best and worst in your behavior?

Use the simple *who, what, and where* model to break down a scene from your day. First think *Who am I? Who am I* to the person I'm talking to? *Who am I* to the group? *Who am I* to the world? For instance, we have our inner feelings and beliefs, and these things fluctuate as we interact and are observed by one person or a group.

What we are doing and where we are also colors our behavior. If I am alone fixing a flat tire, I am stuck because I have weak upper body strength. If a strong man stops by on a deserted road, I can get help, but his character will determine if romance, civility, or danger ensues. If a group of young teens stop by to assist me, they can be comical or they can behave like young heroes. The core *who, what,* and *where* can be useful shortcuts to begin the scene analysis.

Draw upon your own group interactions as you analyze scenes. Think about the different roles you play. I am a mother, wife, vice president of an Emmy®-winning production company, voice actor, author, and teacher. Your role influences your status in a scene. Remember, rank can be fluid too. Don't get stuck with one pattern in your relationship with your scene partner. Start to be aware of your standing in situations in real life. Apply this knowledge to monologue or scene work; just substitute the tangible element of a scene partner and imagine the person is there with you instead.

It's important to note that if you want to be a successful actor, you must practice on your own and with others. When you do a play, you will usually have a lot of rehearsal time with your fellow actors and the director before you perform. On the other hand, when you work on film or TV jobs, you must be prepared to do a scene without as much rehearsal—you must also adapt and react to whatever your scene partner does that you didn't expect to happen. It's advisable, therefore, to learn to perform with other actors in classes or by doing theater.

This can be daunting for an actor because it is time-consuming to meet and rehearse with other performers. It can be challenging to make a living and to find the time to work with others, but this must be done. A writer has a flexible schedule, whereas an actor must find the time to play with others. It is necessary, therefore, to secure employment that supports this lifestyle.

CRAFTING A CAREER

So many actors begin their careers with a variety of goals. Whether you succeed depends on your tenacity and raw talent. Perseverance and innate talent are factors of success or failure, but solid strategies can make a difference. I was inspired to distill some key components of a winning game plan for an actor after watching a brief lecture with John Wooden on PBS. He was the revered basketball coach who led UCLA to so many championship victories. Coach Wooden created a list of key words in his pyramid of success. These traits create a winning game plan in all walks of life.

I realized pertinent words also apply to how actors can reach their professional objectives. These are the crucial concepts to consider as you build your career.

Determination

First, you must want to act. You should have goals and plans you want to fulfill. See yourself doing this and loving it. Aspire to be the best you can be at the craft.

Drive

You must have the tenacity to stick with a career year in and year out, through sickness and health, poverty and wealth, fame and obscurity.

Creativity

Discover ways to keep your imagination fluid and alive. Be playful and explore all kinds of creative adventures to open your mind to new ideas.

Inspiration

Find inspiration in art, life, and your soul to transform words on a page into snapshots of reality. You have to understand human behavior and be able to bring new insights to classics and modern classics alike.

Perspiration

This is the one we all know from our physical workouts. It applies to acting too. Honestly, I usually sweat when I am acting. Under the lights, it can be hot. Physical energy can make you perspire and pure adrenaline can as well. You have to work as hard on a part as you do on your abs.

Generosity

You must share your emotions with an audience and you need to give your full support to every cast and crew member. You have to take direction and be a team player. You also need to be open to another actor's communication of emotions and needs. Your partner gives and you take. Whether it's opening your body to physical touch, or your heart to unexplained moments, you must give everything you can.

Talent

This is something that is innate and it is raw. However, like raw sugar, it can be refined into something sweeter. Some people are born with enormous talent that they share with ease. Perhaps they can look at a page and learn lines with the blink of an eye. Other people may have to work at everything they do. They may have to go over and over their lines or analyze a script from many angles before a part comes to life.

Exceptionally talented actors must be as sensible as those who work hard to achieve the same results. Drugs, alcohol, greed, and ego can rob the most gifted actor of an Academy Award®. Clean living, talent, hard work, and an open heart, though, can earn you an Oscar® too.

Humor

Learn to laugh at life and yourself. Levity brings relief from everyday troubles and adds high notes to your acting. It also feeds your creativity and gives you another perspective on life.

Spirit

Team spirit is the thing that often brings victory above defeat. An actor's spirit is equally important. Plays and scripts are based on life's funny and challenging moments. An actor can't tap into universal truths without a spiritual base. Meditation, religion, and reverence for nature can help us to unearth our mystical roots.

Savvy

I love this word. It means that you're smart about your career. You have a good business sense and don't fall into the wrong crowd. You also know what character type you are and where to market it. In addition, you must understand that you need strong acting techniques and marketing tools. You know that a business requires an investment of time, energy, and funding.

Technique

Acting requires technique just like sports. You must have a fluid strong voice, a pliable body, flexible emotional range, and the ability to analyze and bring parts to life. It takes practice to find the truth beneath the words and to integrate movement into your work. Whether you are doing a role on stage or for the screen, you must learn the tricks of each trade. On-camera work requires subtle movements, while the stage demands demonstrative stances. Just like hitting a ball or making a field goal, skill comes with repetition and strong coaching.

Adoration

Love is at the root of most human endeavors. It's what we fight for, die for, and desire. We must revere our craft and understand the depth of its power in human interaction. We must want to act so much that no one or nothing will stop us from the pursuit of our art.

Passion

Like spirit, passion comes from our soul. At the core of this is a positive attitude. You want to act because you find it fun and rewarding. Passion about the craft will keep you working at your scene from take 1 to take 100 because you know that art can always be refined. You keep a playful attitude and you enjoy the creative process.

Concentration

You need to be able to focus on the scene that unfolds in real time and act. In this day and age, we are so wired this can be challenging. It's becoming more and more difficult to slow down and concentrate moment to moment. We have so much that we do at once. A performer, however, must train like an athlete to let go of the ticking clock. Olympic skater Apolo Ohno discussed this in TV promos for the Olympics. He said that when he is in the *zone,* time slows down and he's fully engaged in the skating. An actor, too, must learn to find an intense concentration that is quiet and worry free. This takes practice and relaxation. Try to find ways to let go of everyday problems when you work. Use whatever meditative techniques help you reach this focused way of performing. Juggling, meditation, and tai chi can be helpful tools for this. Also, as you keep practicing, learning lines, and creating characters, you'll become more proficient at performing roles.

Authenticity

You have to draw on truthful emotions in acting. Audiences don't accept lies or believe phony characters. You must be emotionally connected to your work and create credible roles.

Energy

A car can't run without gas, and an actor can't function without vitality. Nutrition, rest, and fitness can add to your energy. This perhaps can be challenging if you have to rehearse a play, work full time, and then perform. However, you must find the strength to be a captivating actor.

Balance

Falling is easy; standing on one foot for an extended time takes practice. Actors must work from a center that is in harmony with their life so that they can be creative when they perform. Planning ahead to save money for classes and to find flexible jobs that allow you to do time-intensive theater performances can help. It's all about integrating everything in your life so that you can also enjoy it. If you are emotionally unstable because you aren't doing what you want, then you have to review your goals and set a new course to reach them. You must pinpoint what you need to do to make your life better—even if you have to take a break from acting to realize how much you love it.

Conviction

Actors must be convinced they can succeed and be totally committed to the roles they play. This comes with three components: heart, body, and soul. Actors must believe in their heart that they are doing the right thing. They must draw emotions from their soul to create credible moments. This, in turn, will translate into movements and expressions through the body.

If performers can commit themselves to the craft with heart, body, and soul, they should feel confident. They should also understand that performing is ultimately an act of sharing. It's important to give your gifts to others. So a casting session or performance no longer becomes angst-ridden, but rather it is a display of generosity of your spirit.

If you believe in what you are doing because you are prepared and committed to your character, then you should want to share it. You should be glad to help directors and writers bring their vision to life. You should believe in your talent and have faith that you will find a part that is perfect for you to play. If you don't believe in yourself, you can't perform well. Doubt clouds your creative spirit and robs you of truthful work. Confidence comes with experience, the support of others, talent, and the culmination of hard work. If you are lacking confidence, then you must examine what is missing in your acting arsenal before you can succeed.

Sometimes therapy may be required to help you trust your instincts. Do whatever is necessary to help you believe in what you are doing, because all acting is pretending. Acting is about concentrating all of your efforts and transporting yourself into a fantasy world that an audience will also believe in and watch with bated breath.

HOME ACTING PLAYBOOK

1. Rehearsing with a scene partner is always helpful in preparing for a role. Think about people you can call on to practice acting scenes with even when you aren't auditioning. Have a buddy system in place. If you are being considered for an important role, however, always seek the help of a professional coach if at all possible. As an alternative, barter with a strong acting buddy to be coaching partners if you can't afford a qualified coach.

An objective eye can always help you keep your work fresh and modify awkward choices. Don't work alone—build a community of acting partners even if you are working on a monologue. It's very easy to work in a vacuum and lose sight of pacing and unclear choices when you are performing solo.

2. Make a list of times when you are lost in thought and not responsive to a friend. Write or record your inner monologue. Consider how you feel about the person trying to communicate with you.

Conversely, recall times when you desperately wanted to talk to someone and the person was lost in thought. How did that change your behavior? What interior dialogue was going through your mind?

Select a scene that is right for you and use the aforementioned observations to create barriers between you and your scene partner.

3. Remember those perfect moments when you and a friend or a lover clicked? List the events and moments that made it happen. Distill this into the *who, what, and where* element. Find a parallel scene and act as if you are recreating one of your own personal scenes that you experienced.

4. We all snap in life. Think about the times when you did this in public. Reenact your scene. Recall how a person or situation was a trigger for your tirade. Now improvise how a person watching you reacted to your tantrum.

Reflect upon a time when you were berated by a boss or friend and remember how you reacted. Decide if it was justified or unjustified and how that determined your reactions. Integrate aspects of these life lessons into appropriate scenes.

5. Do a timeline that leads to a break up of someone close to you like a lover, acting teacher, or friend. Analyze the events that unfolded and your reactions and feelings to the event. Draw on these experiences for an *as if* exercise with an appropriate scene you find. Use these observations for scenes that you practice and perform.

6. Think of a family member. Recall three pivotal moments with that family member that you remember vividly. How does your relationship grow and change in this instance? What are your expectations of the person and what is expected of you? For example, we may want to please a domineering parent. Dig deep and think of an event when you changed the dynamic of the relationship. Observe or play with a scene where you could use what you've learned about your turning point in a relationship.

7. Consider what it takes to go up and down with another individual on a seesaw. If the other person is heavy, you have to push more or vice versa. Nonetheless there are moments when that dynamic teeter-totter pattern shifts. Start to be aware of the seesaw effect of interactions you have and how a real-life scene changes as you get what you want or you yield to someone else's needs. Be open to this ever-changing flow when working with a scene partner in practice scenes.

8. Find someone to use as a partner even if the person isn't an actor. Learn to do a scene full out with a nonactor so that you know what it is like to work with a reader who gives you little back. Know what your opposite character wants and needs and how that affects your objectives, and do a scene as if you are working with an actor who will give you something dynamic to work with. This is great preparation for actual auditions where anything can happen.

Remember, you have to know your scene partner's lines and motivations to really imagine how a scene would actually unfold. Directors want to hire actors who know a scene so well that they don't need an exceptional audition reader to bring the performance to life.

9. Find a short interview in a magazine. Pick a part you will do and practice it, saying the questions or answers as if you are responding to a real person. First, record the other person's lines and leave enough space for you to say your lines. Next, practice reading your part with the tape. Do both the part of the interviewer and interviewee to get a sense of two different points of view. Notice how the recording helps with your listening skills. Then practice without the tape and use your imagination. Note the difference between the two characters. An interviewer has an overall objective to get information and must listen to the answers. On the other hand, an interviewee has to listen carefully to the question and answer it spontaneously. Use this exercise to sharpen your listening and improvisation skills. It can help you prepare to be receptive even if you perform with a passionless reader at an audition.

10. Select a script from a collection like the *99 Film Scenes for Actors* book or find a buddy to help you transcribe a scene. Practice your part alone, imagining you are performing with your partner. Get a video copy of the film scene. Find the section you have worked on and fast-forward to your partner's first line. Pause the video and play the cue line from the actor in the film. Say your part and pause the recording. Try to pick up on the kind of energy you'd need to do a scene with a celebrity and use that as you work on your auditions in the future. If you can scan the video, continue using the star as a *scene partner* to cue your response on each line. Just make sure that you create your own acting choices and don't copy the actor doing your part in the film.

11. Even if you don't sing, find a favorite song. Usually you can download lyrics on sites like http://lyrics.com/ or http://new.music.yahoo.com/lyrics. Think about the lyrics as a monologue. Create a scene that leads you to speak or sing your lines and also decide who your scene partner is.

Look at the lyrics of a duet song like "Baby, It's Cold Outside" or "Anything You Can Do." Study the dynamic of the two characters. Note how easily they mesh and also notice where there is tension. Balance and counterbalance like this comes into play in scenes too. Reflect upon this kind of connection when you work with partners.

STUDY THE STARS

▶ Romantic Partners to observe through time: Bogart and Bergman in *Casablanca,* Tom Hanks and Meg Ryan in *You've Got Mail*, and Katherine Heigl and Seth Rogen in *Knocked Up*.

▶ Partners Against Crime: See the different interactive styles of Detectives Stabler (Christopher Meloni) and Benson (Mariska Hargitay) on *Law & Order: SVU* or Sam (LL Cool J) and "G." (Chris O'Donnell) on *NCIS: Los Angeles.*

▶ Watch the group dynamic of ensemble actors in action movies, sitcoms, and procedural dramas. Study how each character assumes a role to help define the group dynamic and contribute to the plot development.

▶ Media Resources: Go onto a matchmaking Website to see how people present themselves to potential romantic partners. Focus on a type that you might play. Then create a character and improvise a monologue about the person.

▶ Think about how different patterns of movement would influence your scene. Search for clips and observe the synergy of classic dance couples like Astaire and Rogers and contrast it with the less honed timing of contestants on *Dancing with the Stars*. Use this to understand the kinds of comfortable or clumsy movements you may have with male or female partners in a scene.

▶ Study scenes with fencing, or other combat choreography to explore conflicts you might encounter with a character. Consider how you would choreograph the movement of your scene and think about how your proximity to your scene partner would affect the dynamics of your scene.

▶ Don't forget to practice your tongue twisters to be ready for anything. Refer to the appendix to find exercises, but make sure to do a vocal warm up before you practice.

Getting Started–
Finding Yourself

In an audition, an actor is on his own when he does a monologue. There is no scene partner and there may be no props or set dressing to stimulate the imagination. As noted, even if an actor is auditioning with sides, the casting director or reader is not like a connected scene partner. Readings can be flat or uninspired. A performer, therefore, must learn to create a scene that seems real in challenging circumstances.

Monologues are used as a test of skill for many reasons. First, the piece may help a director decide if the actor can portray a character for a particular role. It can also be a performance scene that demonstrates acting range for an agent, director, or theater company. Whatever the reason, an actor must showcase proficient skills in a short time span.

None of this will be daunting if you truly prepare for the part and rely on a fully charged imagination. You must focus and concentrate on real things in a place where there may be no peace and quiet. The character's overriding objective must fuel the delivery of the lines, so you can't help but say the speech. The monologue or scene has an energy force that is almost like lava flowing from a volcano. It is something bubbling, seething, and ready to erupt.

First, you must decide what causes the eruption. Devise a chain of events that sets up the scene. Discover what triggers this heartfelt delivery of words. Is it anger, pain, love, or fear? How will this speech relieve the mounting pressure that the character feels at a particular point in time?

Often, it's helpful to think of a monologue as a dialogue and to decide who is your scene partner. You may, in some instances, be having a dialogue with yourself rather than with another person. Even if it is self-reflective, it still may be useful to rehearse this like a dialogue to another character that represents a different part of you. In either instance, you do not actually perform the scene with a scene partner, so you have to imagine the person, or strong internal persona, is present with you because it can help you to be more spontaneous. Herein lies the challenge.

If you are in a scene without another actor present, you have to visualize how he reacts to your words and, in turn, how you adapt your speech to the subtle cues your partner exhibits. You can even conjure up what is said between your lines in your rehearsal to create more authentic acting choices. Play with it as if it is a dialogue to get a tangible interplay. So if the line is "I don't want to go out," I might imagine my fellow performer said, "Let's go to dinner."

This is necessary because acting replicates spontaneous, fluid behavior. It should be flexible and ever changing, just as we are in our everyday lives. An actor unfortunately has a script, so she already knows what will be said and she must create a world that is full of change with an array of rich details that mimic real-life situations. For example, the thespian may summon sounds, memories, and facial cues of an imagined person, real-life events, or inner emotions fueled by a backstory to create a real-life scene.

It can be a relief if there is a colleague in a scene feeding a performer lines and creating a flow of mood changes. However, there are no helpers when a thespian is alone saying a soliloquy. An actor must perform as if he is a character in a precise place with an extreme need to express something to a specific person. In addition, the actor must decide why it is so important to share this information with the imagined character or, in some cases, to express inner thoughts out loud.

This can be a very uncomfortable experience if the performer slips out of the fantasy world into a reality where a director or agent may be waiting impatiently to move on to the next audition. Playing it safe and sticking to a script like a child reciting a poem will not help either. The words must flow naturally. Many tools can be used to fill your mind with suitable triggers, but a successful performance only can occur when you let go and work from one moment to the next just as we do in everyday life. Finding an age-appropriate character that suits your type can be a good start to ease tensions. In order to do this, you need to know who you are first.

KEEP SEARCHING FOR CLUES

Consider why you want to act. Create your own monologue about why you want to become an actor. What moment made you throw caution to the wind and do it? Who influenced your decision most? Who was against you? You can write your monologue or rehearse it as a speech. Take your time and get wrapped up into saying this speech to an imagined person. Select someone you know well and decide why this is information that you need to share. Make an audio or video recording, if at all possible, to observe how you talk and perform naturally.

Figure out what type you are. Are you the leading man or lady? Do you love *character* parts? Watch a movie or TV show and choose what kind of parts you would play. Ask your friends and family about what type you are. How can you stretch your skills?

Now review real-life situations to find where you fit into scenes. Are you the fun person at the party? Do you prefer intimate dinners at home? Are you a contentious, demanding person who always has to be in control? How would you introduce yourself in different situations? Do a pretend job interview for a range of employers. What information do you share or withhold?

Change your situation to an office party. Are you friendly and open or guarded? Do you drink and get silly, or are you always sober and in control? Review a week and then a whole year of major events in your life and examine how you adapt and react naturally in a range of situations with different people and in diverse places. Draw on these observations to make choices for various roles you devise. Take a simple monologue and pretend you are saying it to someone from your own life who you have analyzed. Enumerate how you are different and similar to the character.

Keep exploring your range while finding roles that are close to your type. By observing your everyday life and reflecting on your past behaviors, you will begin to build an array of characters you may play. On the other hand, you can have fun exploring roles that are a stretch too. Observe people and then go home and play a character you watched. Do a spontaneous monologue based on a person you have observed.

Study celebrities from TV, the Web, and movies. Make a list of your favorite stars. Specify reasons why you like these celebrities. What strengths can you draw on from their performances? Figure out what things make you uneasy when you perform. Understand how professional actors overcome these obstacles. Watch *Inside the Actors Studio* and read books by your favorite stars to learn their tricks.

Also, begin to embrace your own traits. Keep in mind that you are unique and no one can play you. Therefore self-discovery is an important part of showcasing your talent. Be comfortable with who you are and know that your talents are as valid as any other performer as long as you can uncover genuine and heartfelt moments that are universal to everyone. Reflect on times when you feel in control and confident. Use those traits to empower your auditions.

You may need to work on your focus and concentration skills to deflect distractions away from your scene. Find meditative tools that can sharpen your technique.

Practicing your craft alone at home, in classes, and with a friend or family member is important too. Performance skills will improve only if you put in the effort. Too many performers feel entitled or owed a part and let their technique get rusty. Those people are often called unemployed actors.

IMITATION VERSUS CREATION

So many voice actors tell me they are great imitators. That's always interesting to learn. Basically they are saying they have a good ear and can parrot vocal intonations and characters. It's one tool a performer uses to create roles. However, actors often must start from scratch and not rely on existing roles as templates.

Here are some exercises to explore your imitative and inventive skills. First, find a script or have a friend transcribe one for you from a current TV program that you don't watch. You may be able to download scripts for a minimal onetime fee on Websites like Showfax.com.

Second, select a role that is right for you and rehearse the part as if you are auditioning for it. Even memorize your lines. If possible, perform and record it. Do an audio recording if you can't record the visuals. Save this and then compare your work to the actor who plays the role on TV. Evaluate your performance and decide if you could have booked the part. List the things the TV performer did that you didn't and vice versa. Continue to do this exercise to learn about how you can expand your creative process.

You can do the same things with commercial monologues. Come up with a list of products that match your personal style. Have a friend transcribe some commercial copy that matches your strengths and then compare your work with the professional on TV. Conversely, imitate another actor while watching the commercial in real time. In other words, use the *mirror chat* improvisation exercise. Try to say the words as quickly as you can to imitate the other actor's style. Then right away do an improvisation of the commercial, imitating the other performer.

Evaluate the differences of mere imitation and your fresh creation of roles. Refer to this to detect moments when you are not fully engaged with your performances. Sometimes it's easy to push a performance and be superficial if you are just imitating another person. As you experiment with different media examples, also take note of different styles of acting for commercials, procedural TV dramas, and comedies. Every style comes in handy as you attempt to make a living as an actor, so start to become aware of all the different nuances.

Finally, select a few monologues from your favorite stars and imitate their work. Then uncover roles you haven't seen these actors perform and acquire a script for the part. Practice the monologue and compare your interpretation with the celebrity's performance. What important things have you left out of your work? What does the star add to the part that you don't? Determine if this is a good character for you or not. Specify the choices the celebrity makes that you need to incorporate into your own performances.

YOUR TYPE

Typing or figuring out roles that match your unique style is one way to select performance pieces that can showcase your best talents.

Create a detailed account of the roles you play in your life. Include occupations, family roles, and character traits. Ask friends to tell you what kind of commercial roles or TV characters you could play. Get specific. Are you the victim or the killer?

Certainly your looks dictate the kinds of parts you'll play. Leaf through magazine ads to discover a good match to your type. Flip through commercials and identify roles that you might play. Get a good compilation scene book or monologue book and read a range of scripts out loud one time. Make note of the characters that feel natural and easy and those that are difficult for you. Examine why some are a perfect fit and others aren't. Do you need to open yourself to more of your own life experiences, or do your physical traits contribute to the incongruity? Continue to work at stretching yourself and searching for types that match what an audience wants to see you play.

Record or switch to different kinds of TV shows and imitate different characters. Start to figure out what feels right. Do you find it easy to play a doctor or lawyer or both? What occupations are effortless and which ones are uncomfortable? Write down your observations. Find characters that stretch your type as well as those you can easily play. Of course you may want to pursue parts that are well within your range if you are just starting your career because you'll have so many things to learn before you may feel at ease performing professionally.

HOME ACTING PLAYBOOK

1. Endow a space you are in with an event from the past. Recall the memories and emotions you had during the event. Remember what circumstances led you to this moment. See the details of the space in front of you where the fourth wall is. (It's the space that is between you and an audience when you perform.) For example, see windows, curtains, vases, or whatever was in the space. Let the space, memories, and emotions meld together and remain dynamic.

For example, I can recall very vividly when my husband won an Emmy. As I see the stage and recall the audience, my heart pounds with anticipation and excitement.

Select some other occasions that may have created sadness or happiness. See the details of the space in your mind's eye and let your emotions evolve with ease. Focus on as many details of the incident as possible. Then create a soliloquy about the situation and perform it. Also, find a solo script that matches the mood of one of your past events and practice it.

2. Think about and create a monologue for a scenario you've experienced in the past such as a job interview, marriage proposal, or breakup. Focus on the situation. Mull over the many decisions you had to make. Then tell it to a mirror as if you are saying it to a friend or relative. The key here, however, is not to look at yourself—but to see a space and a person in front of you. Fight the narcissistic tendency to check yourself in the mirror. If this is too difficult, say it to a blank wall first.

Now say the aforementioned monologue as you are going through your closet looking for the perfect thing to wear while you imagine you are talking to someone. Focus on finding exactly what you want to wear. Go back and forth between searching for the outfit and talking to your invisible scene partner. You don't have to stick to a script. Feel free to improvise your speech. You should feel freer as you add movement to your work.

3. Sit in a chair as if it is in a church, school, or office. Let your body mold to the space that you are picturing in your mind. Walk in this space. Adapt to your surroundings. Laugh in the space.

Next, recall an incident you experienced in a space in which you had a strong interior monologue. Then pretend that you are saying this to someone you wanted to tell it to in the past or express it out loud if it was solely an internal dialogue. Decide why you are delivering this speech. Do you say it to relieve your guilt, to share your disbelief, to confess, or to complain about something? Analyze your choices and come up with a strong overriding objective that propelled you to say it.

4. Look at yourself when you are relaxed and unaffected. Now take on some physical traits of someone you know. Imitate the person and really transform yourself. Mold your face and movements to match the person's gestures. Do you see your character transformation? Can you create a truthful monologue for your character without being broad or false? Every actor has a certain amount of range. Some performers play characters very close to their type while others can portray a wide array of roles. What kind of breadth do you have? Remember to build an honest, authentic character with real wants and desires. Don't play at the part or comment on the character. The trick is to still keep the acting choices real so you don't become too broad or false.

5. Imagine who your scene partner would be for your monologue. Write out what the person would say between your scripted lines. If you are talking to yourself, figure out what your alter persona would say. Record your imaginary scene partner's lines and leave enough space after each sentence so that you have time to deliver your next sentence in the monologue. Then play back the recording and practice doing the scene as if you are working with a partner. Once you've done this a few times, simply rehearse your monologue as it is written and try to imagine your partner or alternative personality is present with you in the scene even though the person doesn't utter a word.

STUDY THE STARS—ACTORS WHO USED PERSONAL EXPERIENCES TO CREATE MEMORABLE CHARACTERS

- Sylvester Stallone in *Rocky*
- Tina Fey in *30 Rock*
- Matt Damon in *Good Will Hunting*
- Lucille Ball in *I Love Lucy*

Media Resources: Study an array of classic characters on AMC (www.amctv.com), Turner Classic Movies (www.tcm.com), TV Land (www.tvland.com), Hulu (www.hulu.com), and consult TV Guide (www.tvguide.com) for retro programming.

3

Understanding
Your Character's Needs
and Conflicts

Working with another actor can be challenging. A colleague may not deliver a line the way you imagine it should be said, or you may actually dislike your scene partner. Some actors can be as isolated working with another person as they are when they perform alone.

These aforementioned examples can be problematic in both instances because a performer must listen intently and respond freely without barriers. He needs to take his time to hear the words, just like in real life when he has to make sense of something new. An actress must think about how this new information affects her wants and needs at that moment and then speak to her scene partner. By taking the time to listen and respond, an actor can begin to work moment to moment.

It is often said that the words mean nothing in acting. This can be demonstrated by a response to a simple line like "Good evening." That line can be accompanied by a million different emotions depending on what that character's desires are at a given moment. For example, if Mr. Darcy in *Pride and Prejudice* utters this line to

Elizabeth right after she learns that he has betrayed her family, she will be livid. If he says the same line later in the classic story after he has rescued Elizabeth's sister from disgrace, however, she will gush like a schoolgirl.

Remember, the words are like hot coals and you should tread on them lightly. It's the fire beneath the words that creates the fluid changes in our behavior. An actor must make the appropriate choices for what lies beneath the words, whether she is playing a scene or performing a monologue.

This, however, does not mean that your choices won't change. As you perform a play, you will gain fresh insights. This will create new and perhaps more complex motivations for your character. It is shortsighted to believe that there is a perfect way to interpret a role. That is especially true of many students who study voice-over. They become very tense because they want to do it perfectly, when in fact the opposite approach would yield more fruitful results. Intuitive emotions arise when you allow yourself to breathe and relax and react like you would in a real-life situation. The words can get in the way too often because they allow us to shut down and protect ourselves from exposing sincere, authentic, and vulnerable moments. They can also tempt lazy actors to make no emotional choices at all.

Keep in mind that we often don't listen to others in life, so a solo scene is challenging for an actor who hears a partner deliver a monologue. How often in life have you tuned out when a friend spews a long tirade? Consider how you reach out to have someone really hear what you're saying. You constantly check in for some kind of feedback—use this as you imagine seeing a scene partner's reactions.

In the case of expressing a true internal monologue, figure out why you are saying it out loud. Do you talk to yourself rarely or only when you're under stress? Recall times when you've uttered an internal speech and find ways to use your own experiences when you do a soliloquy. You may often utter an internal dialogue to weigh two sides of an issue, such as "to be or not to be" in Hamlet. In some instances, you play three roles: that of the speaker, listener, and audience all at once. Consider these levels as you rehearse a soliloquy that is not directed to another actor.

An actor must, therefore, react freely when performing a monologue or scene just like in life, and not feel rushed to utter the next line. It's very helpful to imagine you are saying the soliloquy to one person because you can create a tug-of-war of emotions as you imagine your partner's response to your lines. Of course, you won't actually wait that long to hear a response when you perform. You have plenty of time, however, to experiment freely in your rehearsal process to analyze why you need to connect to the other character.

EXAMINE YOUR INTERACTIONS

This process can be simplified if you consider how you interact with your own friends. For example, what kinds of things do they say to trigger various reactions from you? How do you behave differently in a variety of group interactions? Observe how your status fluctuates with different people.

Think about your emotional investments in your relationships. Are you more temperamental with one friend than another? Are you calmer with a different friend? Be aware of how your surrounding space defines and determines your behavior. For example, you generally are quiet and courteous in a church. In contrast, think about what situation would cause you to go berserk in a house of worship.

Also, begin to be aware of how high the stakes are for you in different interactions. A wedding, funeral, or graduation can bring forth a well of emotions as a result of the situations that led to each specific milestone event. There can be feelings of loss or joy or both at these events. A job interview can be tense, but the stakes are much higher if your wife is pregnant and the stock market just crashed. Obviously, a scene is more interesting if there is an intriguing backstory beneath the words.

Acting mirrors the very essence of everyday life. Performances are born from one person's journey through a labyrinth of twists and turns of conflicts and resolutions. If the performance is credible, the audience believes that they are experiencing this for the first time, just like in life. There is a cause and effect element to acting that is necessary to produce a replication of real-life spontaneity. An actor must recreate realistic moments in spite of an unnatural setting and a planned script. Reactions must not seem rehearsed. Emotions must flow in real time so that authentic and unplanned responses can be created.

BE AWARE OF ACTIONS AND REACTIONS

The rehearsal process is a way to hit your mark, go over your lines, and move creatively in the space. It's a time of free exploration, but a performance must be linked to a logical course of events. I will use some simple analogies to illustrate the point. If you think of a person or character like a pinball at rest, that is the beginning of life. Suddenly the forces of nature push on the ball, and it reacts to every new angle. Those reactions are like actions that lead to emotional responses in life. We humans behave based on our upbringing, environment, and the course of events in our lives.

We are on one track until something bumps us onto another direction. In acting, that may be commonly thought of as a *beat* change. For instance, first we get up to get coffee so we can wake up. We exchange pleasantries with a spouse, but then the phone rings and a parent tells us she can't cover the carpool. There is a beat change. Initially, we get up just to get coffee and wake up. We change our whole course of action, however, after the phone call. We may wake up relaxed and happy, knowing we don't have to drive a half hour before we begin our work, but then we become excited and maybe anxious and annoyed as one more thing is added to our day, or we may be elated to spend extra time with our child. The choices are defined by the character type and life history.

A different example would be between a husband and a wife on an anniversary. The wife waits with love and expectation as she plans to broach the subject of having a child. At dinner, the husband unexpectedly reveals he has had an affair. Suddenly love turns to hate, regret, and sadness. The passions emerged from a chain of events. Therefore, I must be clear that if I mention emotions in this book, it is in this context. There is a chain of events in every character's life that will play a role in shaping the reactions and emotional fluctuations within a scene.

Don't forget the big picture. The terrain we travel, the relations we have with others, and our own goals shape our responses. Also, the past often comes alive in a scene. If your character has been abused, she may shun sex. Just like a great marathon runner faces an important race at the Olympics, a character often encounters very crucial moments in his own life; all the people and events that have preceded him determine whether he falters or glides along. If a marathon runner gets injured, the drama of the race is heightened; can he overcome it?

We, the audience, watch with great anticipation for the outcome much in the same way we are drawn into comedies and dramas—we wonder, how will this end? We experience circumstances and emotions that mirror our own lives and feel catharsis, empathy, or relief. It is a release for all of our own pent-up feelings.

We look to the future and anticipate our dreams. It is where our hope or dismal failure lies. Will there be a marriage? Will this person live? In soap operas, dramatic moments are heightened as death threats, disinheritances, and betrayals abound.

The challenge of the actor is to design a life story and backdrop for a character that is logical and believable. It is not only about recreating emotions. It is also about devising a network of actions and reactions that produce the feelings.

So, just like a pinball, we are jostled, stopped, and catapulted places. In the monologue, we will land somewhere important like when a ball hits a spot that lights up. As we work on our part, we need to understand what we want and need and why it is important to us. We must reflect on a past life, consider the ways others influenced and changed our current circumstances, and then grasp the forces that guide us to our end point. If the pinball were a person, it would want to hit a jackpot. In most cases, so do we.

Consider the lengths we go to get things in life. We want to be rich instantly without working for it, so we may even steal to gain a fortune. We hope to find love, especially if we never were loved as a child. I used many sports analogies in my voice-over book, and may use a few in this book, too, because games are clear; there is a precise goal. Hit the ball over the fence. Make a field goal. Score two points. All an actor has to do is to understand the character's goals, playing field, and what kind of player he is. Does he cheat, or is he a beloved hero we cheer on because he runs with a broken foot and still wins the World Series?

EXPAND CHARACTER CHOICES

Characters are as varied as our favorite athletes. The actor's goal is to capture the essence of what the writer and director envision for a part. Initially, a performer has basic details about a role in a script and is given creative guidance by the director and writer, but then the actor must forge a believable individual by delving into truthful observations of life.

We all have our own distinctive traits. In fact, our DNA shows this. If we leave a strand of hair at the scene of a crime and we've murdered someone, we may be caught. It's truly amazing when you think of how many individuals inhabit the earth.

Keeping this in mind, an actor has lots of characteristics to draw on to create a part. These choices can be refined by the clues a writer and director give us as we work on a role. There are also broad types we can think about, such as a neurotic bookworm, a ruthless killer, or a narcissistic, sexy, young woman. Moral codes and choices made in a life can also shape the part. Bette Davis demonstrates this poignantly as she endears us to an alcoholic street peddler in *Pocketful of Miracles*.

Types are useful in understanding a part but they should not overshadow choices that will produce a unique memorable character. For example, Marlon Brando's *The Godfather* is unique despite the mobster type. Always draw from a myriad of options to create a distinctive mix of traits for a role. If you see the performance as part of an ever-changing interaction with the life in real time, it will be easier to keep it spontaneous and always evolving too. If you set up a monologue with a very important person in your character's life, it will come alive. You must, however, delve into your imagination to create the other person's physical cues. We'll explore more about this in future chapters.

We frequently want to have a one-track mind in life. Our objectives are often as simple as getting ready for work, asking for a raise, or passing a test. Many things will bump into us and divert our path. As we react to actions, behaviors, and physical roadblocks, we will adjust and adapt our thinking and choices. Different beats or changes in direction will send us on another path. An actor must define objectives that are suitable for a part. For example, a casual line like "Here's your pizza" may be free and easy. An audience may just want to see the actor pass through the scene and move the action forward. You can create a vivid life for your character but your goal is simply to drop off a pizza. Actors should understand how their character serves the story and not embellish a part for egotistical or unfounded reasons.

An actor's overall objective is like a theme to a story; it has an arc that extends from beginning to end. A monologue or scene often reflects this mind-set in the same way. A character may lose an object or regret actions taken as they try to reach an objective. A monologue presents a moment to slow down and take everything in, because our lives have a confluence of things coming at us all the time. There are sensual stimuli, physical spaces, people's feelings, and thoughts. Somewhere in the midst of great multisensory experiences, we manage to focus on something for a special reason.

For example, we are very intent on our tasks in sports or while we are drawing a picture. There are also intense interpersonal moments that force us to concentrate. Plays and stories expose these times in our character's lives and the monologue and audition scene may explore the most illuminating moments in the entire script.

We are never really alone in a monologue or when auditioning in a scene, because we are intensely connected to our scene partner or alter persona as we uncover new thoughts. Our emotions will fluctuate as we react to events that have happened or might occur. New thoughts are based on a myriad of experiences and emotions. The soliloquy or critical scene is often an important turning point that will take us to another big beat change. If you think about it, little beats bring us to this point, and new ones will emerge until we face another moment of clarity.

PRACTICE PAYS OFF IN PROFESSIONAL SETTINGS

The monologue is the gold nugget at the center of a play, movie, or TV program because it solidifies so much for the character and the writer. It is also helpful in a range of professional settings. Kristof Konrad is an L.A. actor with credits including *Angels & Demons, Independence Day, Hotel California, Nikita, The Agency, JAG,* and *Gilmore Girls.* Kristof is a graduate of the Alexander Training Institute of Los Angeles. He has a private practice in West Los Angeles and is an active member of the American Society for Alexander Technique (AmSAT). Kristof Konrad explains how soliloquies are an integral part of character development for actors. He says, "The monologues are the windows to the most intimate parts of the character's life. They force the actor to work on given circumstances, objectives, intentions, and obstacles. The actor must also discover the emotional need or justification that pushes the character to go forward. All of those elements are absolutely essential for breaking down your script in order to create a believable, living and breathing human being. The monologues are your workout sessions for that."

Voice actor Bob Bergen, who portrays the animated character Porky Pig, describes how relevant monologues are to professional performers. He says, "Doing a thirty second voice-over spot basically *is* a monologue . . . if you are doing a thirty or sixty second commercial you are basically doing a monologue. Same goes for an animation audition. An actor on stage tells a story, a voice actor in a commercial does the same thing, while also selling or promoting a product. Acting technique and monologue work will only enhance the voice actor's craft."

Actors will always study, therefore, and need to showcase monologues, even if they are not used for auditions. As discussed, sample isolated scenes or sides may be used instead of monologues for auditioning purposes. In both instances, scenes are taken out of a full-length script so the performer must fill in the details. The exact specifications of each situation may vary. An actor may have the sides for a few days before auditioning, or in some rare instances, for a few moments prior to testing for a part.

Bob Bergen finds that working on both scenes and monologues is relevant in his profession. As he notes: "Rarely if ever do you have a scene partner present when auditioning for animation. But they are there in the scene. The actor is interacting, even if the scene partner isn't heard. Mistakes many actors make is just reading their lines without any thought of their unheard scene partner, their relationship with them, etc. Monologue work, and acting technique will always come in handy with voice-over."

Whether you're stepping up to the mic or in front of the camera, you'll draw on these skills in everyday work environments. You'll want to be ready to perform anything that comes your way. Observe everyday moments in your own life and start to stockpile events, scenes, and emotionally charged scenarios to draw upon for your work. Notice how you adapt and change to situations as they evolve, and begin to understand how various social interactions and course of events change your wants and desires. Then call on these observations when you work on your monologues or scenes.

BODY AND SOUL

All performers must integrate a character into their body. When you study acting, you become aware of how movements and stances can help you demonstrate your character's underlying desires. You need to be fit to make the most of your physical communication. Exercise and movement classes are essential tools to keep a performer toned. A body must be strong and pliable to bend to the needs of your role.

Moreover, you need to release tension so that creative energy and thoughts can flow freely. Keep in mind, however, that you must be sensible and know your own limits. I can't protect you from harm, so use good common sense. You are responsible for any actions you take, so use good judgment. Find a discipline that is right for you and seek professionals who will guide you properly.

Pilates, yoga, and the Alexander technique can be useful tools. Simple relaxation and meditation can help you to prepare for work too. Generally, you need to become aware of where you hold tension and learn to release it. Auditions can be nerve-wracking, but if you can condition your body to become relaxed and to breathe more fully, you may be able to face your fears with fewer roadblocks.

Physical tension is very visible to audiences. Kristof Konrad observes how actors can betray their work with uptight body language.

"Often, when I see actors performing, I see them being very uncomfortable in their bodies even though they look like they spend their whole life at the gym. They remind me of the stiff telegraph poles on the streets. They are very unexpressive and there is very little life in them."

Kristof Konrad describes how movement training can enable an actor to create powerful performances.

"Your body is your cello that you play on. More then seventy-five percent of your communication happens in your body. You have to learn how to create ease in it, which will free your breath, make you more available to your partner and the circumstances . . . The rigid body is like an armor, which will make all of those connections more difficult. Your body speaks before you speak. If I don't believe your body, I will not believe you."

Therefore, don't neglect your body, breathing, vocal fitness, and relaxation. Start to give a high priority to these areas and don't get lazy. A well-tuned physique can help you create a character stance quickly. If you are out of practice, warm up first and then flip through the channels on TV and mime different body movements. Assume animal poses. Even imitate creatures on nature shows. Don't forget to laugh to release tension. Children's books are great to use as sources of inspiration for broad character movements. Creative work must be free and easy, so train yourself to be ready for any challenge.

BREATH AND VOICE

You must be realistic at auditions. If a scenario is given to you at the last minute, don't panic. See it as a challenging creative game. Tension will only hinder your performance. Proper breathing is essential to commanding vocal work and it also helps you to stay focused on the task at hand.

Also, always do a vocal warm-up so you don't get tongue-tied if nerves kick in at an audition. Singing is a wonderful tool for any actor to explore. You learn to expand your vocal range as well as to protect your voice. Pat Whiteman teaches voice privately, has taught at UCLA Extension, and is an acclaimed performer. She suggests, "Formal voice study can also help actors focus their sound and aid with diction and articulation problems. . . . Singing also assists in relaxing the performer. Tension is the evil of the singer. Ultimately, what we are trying to attain as singers, even in heightened passages of music, is a sense of letting go, freedom and authenticity—qualities that any actor can relate to."

Pat Whiteman also talks about the side benefits of singing.

"I think the most compelling performance strength I see from actors who have singing training is confidence. Mastering singing technique and understanding how to deliver a song effectively builds confidence and, as one actor who has studied with me put it, 'stretches the bravery muscles needed for acting'. . . . Studying voice can also have a pronounced effect on an actor's overall being. One actor told me it enhances his sense of self, which gives him more to bring to a role and the challenge of acting. Another actor I've worked with told me his breath control, phrasing, activation, and focus all improved immeasurably with singing."

Pat Whiteman further explains how working on a song can help actors make new connections in their monologue work.

"A song is, indeed, a monologue. They are essentially inter-changeable. Songs have beginnings, middles, ends, characters, elements of discovery and places to go. I think singing takes the acting process one step further for the actor. The exposure, the heightened nature of the medium, everything is magnified through singing. Singing is essentially *super-expressive*."

You'll also need a strong spirit to stay afloat during the tumultuous times when you want to quit the craft. Spiritual life rafts can help you stay motivated and feed your character growth. Volunteering your acting skills for good causes can be very rewarding too. Also, don't let your ego drive your desires—especially if you have great looks. Physical charms can fade as fast as a rose petal falls off the vine; so don't fall head over heels in love with yourself. Remember, acting is a team effort too.

HOME ACTING PLAYBOOK

1. Think about a situation like in the movie *Titanic*. Who in your life would you save if you could just save one person? As you work on a part, figure out which one person your character would save. Conversely, what character would save you in a role you are working on?

2. Take a monologue you are working on and express it only in body movements, not words. Make this broad as if it is mime and you are communicating it without words. Then sit quietly and imagine saying it to your scene partner while seeing her reactions. Perform as if you are on camera with subtle movements and let your thoughts be stronger then your motions. Finally, do the monologue naturally while trying to focus on why you have to say it.

3. We often don't tell people what we want them to know. Improvise monologues that you would like to say to people in your life. Do three monologues. Next, pick a part you are working on and create at least two monologues you want to say to one or two characters in your life and improvise some speeches. Then, work on a monologue that is written for the character.

4. Think about the course of events over a day or week. Reflect on how a series of incidents changed a relationship with someone in your life. Make a list of all of the feelings you had toward this person before and after the event. Consider your discoveries as you analyze a script or create an impromptu monologue about your real-life observations.

5. Reflect and analyze five big situations that changed your life. Try to find different kinds of events that produced diverse outcomes and produced profound realizations. Maybe you had a tragedy, real romance, betrayal, or triumph. Find monologues where you can use these situations to help you imagine what a character truly feels.

6. A monologue often is about a transformation of a character. Because of a culmination of events, the character suddenly realizes life will not be the same. Use simple words or phrases to express the basic feelings your character has from the start of your soliloquy until the end. For example, you might say: I'm lost, I'm scared, I'm angry, I'm insane, I'm jealous, and I want revenge. Then simply put the character's monologue in your own words. Finally, do the speech as written.

7. Take a monologue you are working on and do it three times imagining you are in different physical spaces. Then say it three times as if you are speaking to three different people. Finally, go back to your original choices and see if you have any new spontaneous moments emerge from your work.

STUDY THE STARS

▶ Watch the flashback scene in *The Curious Case of Benjamin Button* for a great example of how a chain of events can change a person's destiny. Observe the set of circumstances that alter the life course of Daisy, Cate Blanchett's character.

▶ Study the pre-life that leads to the outburst of Daniel Day-Lewis's character as he delivers his famous "I drink your milkshake" speech from *There Will Be Blood*.

◗ Reflect on the conflicts Meryl Streep's character faces in *Sophie's Choice*.

◗ Media Resources: Review the psychological drama that develops on HBO's *In Treatment* (www.hbo.com/in-treatment). Read current stories about individuals' travails in magazines. Reflect on the heightened drama people encounter in soap operas and sports events. Experiment using these high-stakes moments from life in your rehearsals of scenes.

◗ Go to www.psychologytoday.com and study different types. Improvise a monologue about a character you create based on what you've learned. Read about stories of personal transformation in magazines, and think about how you can use this for characters you will work on in the future.

◗ Try to observe the lies people tell. Watch court proceedings. Analyze how people behave who pull media hoaxes such as the balloon boy hoax. Discover how people lie in a variety of real-life scenes with the help of recordings on YouTube or news clips.

4

Subtext, Backstory, and Dramatic Trajectory

A writer sets out a blueprint for the actor to follow to bring scenes and characters to life. It's more like an outline that an actor must flesh out or a line drawing that must be filled in with color. Everything the writer gives you is a clue to playing your part. Some elements of the script are clear truths about the scene and roles. For example, a scene location, time of day, and character description gives you a precise roadmap. You need to glean from a script all the information the writer gives you before you dig deeper so you understand what is happening in the scene and the whole story. Once you've exhausted that search, you can look for other key clues.

The way a person speaks tells you about social class, education, and upbringing. You may need to acquire an accent to fully bring your character to life, but don't worry about this if you're inexperienced. It's more important to work on a truthful performance as you rehearse. You can layer the accent on later, because you don't want to be broad, fake, or pushed at first.

The writer's words also tell you about the sequence of events in the character's life, if you read carefully. There will be facts about the individual's biography. You may find out about a past trauma or defining moment. In order to get the most out of a script, you have to study every detail and decide how it shapes your role.

This can be limited if you only have a *side*, which is a portion of a script or an isolated soliloquy. You will have to be creative and devise a backstory or *hook* that can work for an isolated scene. Take a stab at a strong choice; it can be modified if necessary. For example, as recounted in TV interviews, and noted in an article in People.com, Jason Alexander, who played the role of George on the TV show *Seinfeld,* did a Woody Allen type of character when he first performed the part. Later, he modeled George after the show's creator, Larry David.

You must make some choices that will help you fill in the blanks if you don't have a full script. For example, create important events in your character's life that brought you to this moment: was there an accident or something mystical in the past? Chances are you may be a bit off, but a director can ask you to make an adjustment if you miss the mark too much. Try to get as much information from the style of speech, genre, and overall tone of the scene as possible.

You can also review a previous part you've played and look at an isolated scene or monologue. Think about the clues that you are given in the scene. Compare this to all the information you uncover in the entire script. If you have never studied a whole script, Tennessee Williams offers many clear clues for an actor to discover. Now revisit your isolated scene to dig deeper for anything you've overlooked. Also decide what your imagined scene partner wants and needs in the scene.

Then go beneath the words. Does *yes* really mean *no*? Figure out what your character needs most in this one monologue or audition scene. This is often referred to as the super objective, and if you can define it with an active verb, it helps you to know what your character is fighting for. Is it to plead, to confess, or to praise? You must decide what you want most from your imagined scene partner. You'll also have little objectives along the way, or beats. Tennessee Williams is a wonderful playwright to study because his beats are so clear; you can easily find places where his scenes shift from one topic or thought to the next.

SEARCH FOR DIFFERENT LEVELS

The monologue *That's It* in the appendix has a very clear super objective. I don't even have to tell you what it is. Nonetheless, the character makes many overt mistakes that ruin his chances of getting the part.

The different needs and beats dictate a certain rhythm to a scene. At first, the actor in the aforementioned monologue expresses anger. As the scene progresses, things get silly. You have to take the time to let emotions transform from one to another. Everything has a different tempo and direction. A scene with laughter may be relaxed with one-liner zingers going back and forth, while a scene of confrontation may be loud with fast-flying staccato dialogue.

Inexperienced voice actors often play scenes very flat without a lot of ups and downs because they don't delve beneath the words to unearth the smaller moments. There can be an 180-degree shift in mood and rhythm from the beginning to the end of the scene. It can begin with anger and end in laughter or tears depending on what events transpire in the scene. *Yes* can mean *no* in a scene, because we often say what we think we have to say to someone in life rather than telling the whole truth.

You must understand why a character is hiding the truth from the world. Perhaps it's a scene with a wife and husband, and she says that she doesn't want to get pregnant. Upon further investigation of your scene, you might discover that she has learned that she has lupus disease and is afraid she might pass it on to a child. If you only have an isolated monologue, you would have to explore reasons why you think the wife doesn't want to become pregnant and select one choice that would work best for your scene. In other words, you would have to create a choice without the benefit of the backstory provided by a full-length script.

EXPLORE TIMELINES AND PERSONALIZE YOUR PART

You have to enrich the words with a past, present, and future. You must decide what happened to your character to bring her to this point. Then you need to understand the current needs and future desires of your character. Creating a backstory helps you understand motivations and actions in the present. Defining overall objectives and beats, or thoughts and intentions, helps you to clarify your character's immediate and urgent needs. Speculating about dreams and desires in the future can create a long-term dramatic trajectory.

You must understand what the writer's roadmap is and then you must travel along the path that is given and look for every single clue that is evident in the script. Beyond that, you can also analyze situations in your own life that can mirror your character's dilemma. As previously mentioned, if you can't quite relate to an experience in the script, you'll use the *as if* idea to personalize the part. For example, if I'm playing a character who is a neat freak and I am not, then I have to find something else in my life that makes me compulsive and orderly. I have to behave *as if* this other compulsion is driving me to be a neat freak.

When you rehearse, personalize your part and improvise the monologue as if it were in your own words. Do an *as if* for the whole speech to relate it to your life now. Then put the speech in your character's words. Next, improvise it and don't worry about knowing your lines perfectly. Articulate what your character is really thinking and wanting when you do this exercise. For example, rather than utter, "I don't want to get pregnant," say the line, "I just found out that I have lupus and I could pass it on to our child." This reinforces what you're feeling and wanting to express. Finally, rehearse your part as written and connect to your imagined scene partner.

Remember, an actor's job is to expand upon the script and bring logical and believable character traits to life. The words are only a jumping-off point. An actor must be a good student of human behavior and have a fertile imagination to fill in the missing details in a scene. The depth of the performance will be enhanced by the authentic details that make a soliloquy or scene seem as if it is something that is truly spontaneous.

HOME ACTING PLAYBOOK

1. Pretend your character is at a cocktail party introducing himself to a friend of a friend. Do an improvisation about where you grew up and went to school. Figure out what information your character shares freely. Get out of your head and let your thoughts flow freely.

2. Imagine your character has just hit a car. Figure out how she deals with the situation. What immediate thoughts come to mind? What actions are taken? Decide what caused the accident. Make a pretend phone call for help from the accident and decide whom you call first. Will you hide anything from anyone?

3. Watch isolated scenes from TV shows and films. Write down a character's motivations and objectives. Determine what is happening in the scene, and speculate about the details you don't know about. After you've fully examined the segment, watch the whole story and see if your hunches were correct.

4. Pretend that you are a movie star playing your character. Improvise an interview with the press about your part. Come up with questions that you imagine you would have to answer in your interview. Describe your character for the audience. Talk about why it's an interesting role. Describe the obstacles and funny moments that arose as you worked on it.

5. Take a monologue or a scene from a play or a script and work on the isolated part. Make choices and present your finished audition to a friend or record it. Analyze it once you have read the whole play or script. Make a list of acting choices you can change in the future based on your performance.

6. A page number gives you a critical clue about how you play a scene if you only have a side for an audition. Take a play or script that you have not read and randomly turn to a page and read the scene. Then flip to another page and repeat this action. Do this exercise for scripts that you have read and ones that you have never looked at. You can also stop at random points on recorded TV shows to observe how a character's motivations change. Start to understand how the place in the story shapes your actions and choices so that you can use this key information when you audition. Try to study a range of genres, too, so you can get a broad sense of how a story arc evolves.

STUDY THE STARS

▶ Study a detailed backstory: watch *The Hangover*, featuring Mike Tyson in a comedic cameo.

▶ It helps to see *Quantum of Solace* before viewing *Casino Royale*. Think about characters you interact with in a play or show as having a prequel or a secret life that you must uncover.

▶ Media Resources: Read how writers crafted your favorite stories. Go to Websites featuring interviews with screenwriters such as www.screenwritersutopia.com. Review the prerecorded interviews you can buy from the Writers Guild of America at www.wgfoundation.org or search for conversations with your favorite writers on YouTube.

▶ Observe how real people tell stories in documentaries about a range of subjects. Go to hbo.com, aetn.com, eonline.com, history.com, and pbs.org. Compare these people with man-on-the-street interviewees on the news. Notice how a current crisis changes the way people convey stories. Think about the urgency of a situation when you explore a scene.

5

Character

Finding a perfect soliloquy can take some time. Basically, actors spend their entire careers trying to land the best part. I can't imagine anyone but Harrison Ford as Indiana Jones or Vivien Leigh as Scarlett O'Hara. Some people stretch their range and play against type. Other performers transform themselves. For instance, Dustin Hoffman becomes the title character in *Rain Man*. He gives great attention to every aspect of the character's ticks and mannerisms. The halting speech and aloof body language help us to have empathy toward this vulnerable character. We are totally caught up in his performance.

Think about what stars you admire. List the great parts you'd like to play. Define characteristics you can bring to a role. Are you quirky or serious? What roles have you played in life? Do a timeline of your work experiences. Look in the mirror and figure out what type you can play best.

Recall what kinds of compliments and complaints people have made about you. Make a list of all the things other people have said about you. For example, "You're so pretty, you would never go out with a guy like me." On the other hand, someone may have said, "Hey, Four Eyes, where's my lunch money?"

Has anyone ever said you're like a celebrity? I was always told in college, "You should be an actress." I wanted to be a director, so I didn't pay much attention to it, but I did play parts in film and TV productions when I was in college and graduate school. Strangers have told me that I resemble a wide range of stars through the years.

If no one has ever said you look like a celebrity, ask friends you know if you resemble anyone. My acting coach in New York, Bob Luke, who is featured on the CD that comes with this book, would have students work on a monologue based on which celebrity they resembled. You can do this to get a sense of what kind of material may be a good match for you. Once you select a star, then find a monologue from one of their movies. Try to get a buddy to transcribe a suitable part and then you do the same for them so that you're not too influenced by the star's interpretation of the script. Enjoy making your own choices and don't use the celebrity's work as a crutch.

Also review the traits of some of your favorite characters. List the individual attributes that help create the part. Do a chart where you define the innate and learned physical traits. Are there any great ticks? Olivier talks about coming up with a physical mannerism to help define a character in his book *Confessions of an Actor: An Autobiography*. Perhaps a character winces when nervous or laughs inappropriately like the character Alma in *Summer and Smoke* by Tennessee Williams. The style of someone's walk or the way they eat are manifestations of who they are. You must find appropriate traits to flesh out your particular role. Study your part for every possible unique attribute. Then observe different types in real life for authentic ideas to add to your work.

Another way to explore characters is to read through letters to the editors in newspapers and magazines. Pick a part you would most likely play and create a list of traits you would have. Why do you decide to write the letter? What trigger or situation prompted you to sit down and complain or praise something? Review your character improvisations; do you feel more confident pretending to be a celebrity? Use this confidence when you perform.

REACHING FOR A PART

Nothing is nicer than playing a comfortable role with words that flow easily. However, you also need to learn how to explore difficult parts. I have to stretch my skills all the time when I audition for voice-over jobs. I will get characters that aren't what I'd typically play, but I still have to make the audition believable.

One of the easiest ways to approach these kinds of roles is to dismiss your resistance to do them—actors often set up roadblocks rather than clearing their mind to focus on the task at hand. In improvisation, the foremost rule is *yes, and*. If an audience or fellow actor gives you something, you accept the given circumstances and add more details. For example, if another performer says, "You're so old," maybe respond, "Yes, I am over one hundred years old and I knew President Lincoln intimately." Therefore, you are agreeing that you are old and adding information to the scene.

Give in to *make-believe*. That is the way to succeed at any part. Don't resist it. Women can get very vain and it may be hard to play an older role. Yet it can be fun to play this part. I remember how polite my acting teacher, Eugene Lazarev, was when he told me I was going to play an older woman in an improvisation for his UCLA Extension class. It was a dream come true for me! I had often auditioned for older voice-over character parts, but I yearned to explore a fleshed-out character because I had spent so much time visiting my mother in a nursing home.

I'm not suggesting that I don't put up roadblocks, but I can tell you it's a big waste of energy, and actors have very little free time between survival jobs and working on their craft. Remember to let your precious ego relax and get creative.

It's also important to keep the work truthful. Sometimes when you stray from a comfort zone, you may push and become phony. Resist this. For example, you may become too broad if your character has an accent. The dialect is just layered upon your truthful base. Often, actors will work on the part in a neutral accent first and then add the dialect. It's okay to do the part both ways while you're exploring the script. Just always remember to stay with truthful desires and emotions. Make sure to practice your accent on a range of other materials like reading the newspaper aloud so your speech doesn't have a singsong pattern. Also, personalize the part with *as ifs* that make sense to you, if you feel unconnected to the material. For instance, you may not be a heroine addict, but chances are you can relate to something you're obsessed with in your own life. Use it—be creative. "It's a play, so play," is something my improvisation teacher Paul Sills would say.

IMPROVISE AND BE FLEXIBLE

Jump into an improvisation of everyday situations. Figure out how your character behaves in a bar, at work, or in a variety of social settings. Set up pretend scenes to create a backstory or prior conflict. Make real specific choices. The more you can enrich your environment and your life, the more authentic everything will be for you. For example, imagine the fourth wall of your bedroom down to the cracks in the wall. Devise ten events that just happened right before you decide to speak your mind in your monologue. Make your inner motivations strong and justified in your mind. Improvise or write your thoughts or interior monologue. Fully understand why you have to speak up.

Finally, take direction well. Be flexible and free spirited. Once again this is where improvisation experience can pay off. With improv, you have no script, so you can't plan ahead. You just have to *do* your part. As Sanford Meisner, the noted acting teacher, said, "Acting is the reality of doing." In an improvisation exercise, you are forced *to get out of your head* and act in an instant. Use this idea when you are given direction. Let go of your fear of not pleasing the director. You haven't done anything wrong per se; you are simply not fulfilling his artistic vision. You must trust others and be a team player—especially if you are getting paid to perform. Treat it more as a game in which you are trying to guess the right answer. Get more playful and less protective. Even if you don't get a part, you'll grow from stretching your talents. Those new places you've explored will add fresh insights to characters well within your reach.

Being in the moment simply means adapting to what happens after a sequence of events without preplanning your behavior or censoring yourself. If you can reach this level, then you can work more freely because you'll react on stage when a book drops off the table or on set when an actor improvises dialogue. A pliable actor integrates words with an unplanned array of emotions, actions, and reactions. As an actor becomes more technically proficient, he will be able to juggle more levels of thought. An actress moves freely and can adjust to new direction. A seasoned performer can make spontaneous discoveries based on what a scene partner does and react freely.

MONOLOGUES CAN STRENGTHEN TECHNIQUE

As an actor works on the art of doing monologues, layered elements of performance may become more and more refined. In essence, a rehearsal of a soliloquy is not just practice for a part, but also a way to sharpen techniques if done properly. It is aiming for a greater level of difficulty because it taps into the imagination. The performer must see, hear, and react to a space devoid of people, props, and an appropriate setting. By perfecting this kind of performance, therefore, you can prepare for any number of unforeseen circumstances in a working environment.

For example, a performer may have to fight to deliver dialogue on a rainy sea-swept ship. Perhaps the actor must envision an animated creature as a costar. On stage, there are many challenges that can *rock the boat*. Costars forget their lines, props are misplaced, and audiences may laugh in all the wrong places. In short, practicing soliloquies can be like a fitness program. Is it disjointed or unnatural? The answer lies within the actor's ability to rise above the forces that shut down the imagination. If the performer can be free, then he can embrace the creative work where comedy or drama may emerge.

HOME ACTING PLAYBOOK

1. Refer to the soliloquy titled *Little*. Here is a chance to go back in time and be a child again. Rehearse this monologue and make believe that you are a child again. Don't let the subject matter get you too distracted. Keep your strong super objective in mind. Remember, you want to help your brother. If this material is disturbing to you, pick another monologue that is a stretch for you.

2. Improvise a monologue about yourself as if you are playing a person who is your opposite type. If you're shy, do it as a loud person. If you are heavy, do it as a thin person. Imagine you're a contestant on a game show talking to the audience a little about who you are and why you are playing the game. Improvise this soliloquy as your opposite-type character.

3. Imitate a relative at a family gathering giving a toast or making a speech. Use your family members as an inspiration for parts too.

4. Laugh, cry, and whisper something as a character very different than you. Play with a range of roles with this exercise.

5. Think of your scene or monologue as a comic strip. Sketch key events and then write thought balloons for your character. Add to it while you're working through your rehearsal process. You can even write thought balloons for your scene partner.

6. Use gibberish to free yourself from preconceived notions about a part. Just do your monologue with a total nonsensical speech. Take the burden of memorization or being perfect away. Focus on what your character wants as you do your gibberish. Let your emotions be free and uncensored. Then practice your part again after you play with your gibberish.

7. Try to treat memorization as a separate skill so that you will not become caught up on this alone. I learned this by chance when I decided to learn roles from auditions that I printed out from sites like Showfax.com while I worked out at the gym. My goal was to keep my mental acuity sharper, but I discovered many side benefits.

I found I no longer had to think about beats as much. It was also easier to pick up new material. Try it, make it fun, and memorize everything from commercial ads, to songs, to character parts you'd never play.

Remember that you still have to find the right emotions beneath any words you speak when you perform, however. The aforementioned is merely a mental workout exercise and is not meant for the rehearsal of a role that requires thorough analysis. When you work on a part you will perform, you have to explore what a character wants and needs, but you may be able to be freer in a scene if your memory skills are tuned up. Use this freedom to let your physical space come alive and add new dimensions to your work.

8. Often a character is trying to find a piece of a puzzle to put her life in order. For example, the character Sophie wants to know who her father is in *Mamma Mia!* Define what piece of the puzzle your character is trying to solve and how it plays into the outcome of your scene or monologue.

STUDY THE STARS

▶ Watch a range of dramas on TV. I think of *Law & Order, CSI: Crime Scene Investigation, Grey's Anatomy,* and *Criminal Minds.* Pick a role that would be closest to what you would play. For more character choices, go to your favorite show Websites and study the descriptions of current roles.

▶ Watch *Ferris Bueller's Day Off, Whatever Works,* and *The Office*; find a monologue for yourself that is delivered directly to someone you know. If possible, record it and review it. Compare your work to the pros in the aforementioned examples.

▶ Watch comedies. I like *Two and a Half Men, The King of Queens,* or *30 Rock.* Select characters you would play.

▶ Watch *He's Just Not That Into You* to observe a range of monologues and characters. Devise your own fun speech on a topic that is near and dear to you and deliver it.

▶ Watch *The Informant!* starring Matt Damon. Consider how he uses the accent and appropriate traits to build a believable character.

▶ Media Resources: Use a site that has current TV audition scripts like Showfax.com to become familiar with parts that are cast. Consider what characters would be your best fit. Then watch the shows and see what types are cast in the roles.

▶ Look at notable archetypical characters listed on Wikipedia and other sites referenced in the appendix. Refer to the Web links in the appendix and watch the Academy Award®–winning roles actors have played to explore different archetypes.

6

Genre and Mood

Astyle speaks volumes. In fashion, it sets trends, and in the business world, a tasteful wardrobe can ensure your spot in the corner office. Dressing right for a part can help you to define your character. If you don't have an extensive wardrobe, you can still window-shop. Go to a store and figure out what your character would wear and, while you are there, select a bedroom suite. Let real objects help you to realize the full potential of your role.

Fabrics, furniture, and lifestyles help us show our identity to the world. Money and social class also influence the choices we make. Think about where your character dines. Is it a fast-food restaurant or ritzy steak house?

What about everyday life? Make choices about your character's home, car, and workspace. Also create comparable choices for your role if it is a historical piece. For example, imagine the home life, mode of transportation, and social gatherings of the period. These things together all shape how you play your part.

In the same way, a genre dictates an overall tone for a piece of writing. If you are playing a part from a film noir script, you will probably have a shady past and may have a furtive love affair. Lighting will be dark and shadowy to heighten this deceptive world. Of course, in the classic Hollywood movies, characters smoked countless cigarettes and drank heavy liquor fast and furiously.

On the other hand, in a romantic comedy, you may wear your heart on your sleeve in hopes of ensnaring a love interest. Your flaws may be on full display to add a comedic touch. Friends rally to your side as you ruminate over your feelings for a potential lover. Emotions are full and they can create funny moments. Tragedy may be the source of humor in a romantic comedy, but it can lead to murder in a film noir piece. The two genres are almost at opposite ends of the spectrum.

You should always pay attention to an overriding style, but you shouldn't let it distract you from understanding the gut feelings of your character. The genre may dictate the pace, mood, and settings for your scene, but your inner truth must remain strong and sincere.

It's always useful to study different genres so you become familiar with the benchmark styles to help imagine appropriate wardrobe and prop selections. Don't, however, become too broad unless a comedy role calls for it. Define the world and believe you belong in it. Do the same for TV shows and commercials if you want to work in these areas.

Avoid playing everything on one note. Remember there are funny moments in dramas and poignant scenes in comedies. Try to get as many different emotional nuances out of your part as possible. A genre, like an accent, should heighten the work, not smother it.

REVIEW A RANGE OF GENRES

Explore scripts from different styles to find your best fit. If you are a smoldering hot blonde, you could play a femme fatale in a film noir piece. Start to get a sense of your types for both dramas and comedies. Comedies can be very physical with pratfalls and pranks, so it's good to be loose and easy. There is also a cadence to a setup and punch line that must flow. On the other hand, a dark-rooted confession of a character like Mildred Pierce played by Joan Crawford can have a fierce intensity and dramatic crescendo. At first, the body language may be guarded and tense and then shift to being slinky and voluptuous when moments of deep sexual attractions are exposed.

As you explore different styles, learn what your weak points are. Consider ways of overcoming your obstacles. Maybe an improvisation class can help improve your comedy work. Perhaps a Stanislavski class will give you a deeper understanding of drama.

As previously stated, I was fortunate to study with Eugene Lazarev at UCLA Extension. Lazarev taught at the Moscow Art Theater School, and he enriched my understanding of Stanislavski. One of the things Eugene focused on in class was Stanislavski's *event and conflict* idea. This concept can help you to think about the chain of events in a character's life. For example, we all have different kinds of situations in our lives that determine the paths we take. In one scenario, we may encounter a simple event: we get a parking ticket. In another scenario, we may come upon a different incident such as a car accident. The magnitude and intensity of the event will determine the conflicts we face and our reactions.

CONSIDER PREVIOUS SEQUENCES AND SCENE PACING

Our character's history will also affect what happens next. This can be useful information for monologue work because you can begin by reacting to something, not starting cold. It's also helpful to think of the moment before or what just happened to your character prior to the scene as you prepare to speak. You cannot warm up while you do a soliloquy; you must start hot. Therefore, you need to be mentally engaged in the scene before you begin your speech.

Meisner discusses this idea in his book *Sanford Meisner On Acting*. He reminds us that we cannot rush on stage reacting to a crisis unless we make that crisis real first. So if I tell my spouse that I've been fired, then I need to imagine everything that led up to that moment. Was I caught embezzling funds? Did I come to work drunk? Was I laid off because I didn't play the game?

My reaction to this event will be tempered by how important it is to me. If I lose my job in the middle of the Great Depression, my family may become destitute. On the other hand, if the stock market is flush like in the 1990s, maybe my pride is hurt.

You must decide what is critical in any scene. Raising the stakes elevates your needs. I always cite the movie *Casablanca* in my class for being such a great script because the risks are greater and greater in each scene. Watch the movie if you haven't; I don't want to spoil it for you.

One of the ways to make the most out of any genre is to take your time and let the moments flow naturally. We don't have a minute to spare in the modern world, but an actor must slow everything down for a scene. Monologues are generally written about watershed times in a person's life. In these instances, we focus on each second that goes by. Have you ever been in a car accident? I remember when my eighth-grade band bus had a crash. Everything was in slow motion. Events and conflicts force us to react with new insights.

A soliloquy often helps us crystallize and clarify things we've been troubled with for a long time. Bit by bit we realize how a situation has changed us or will alter our destiny. In short, we come to grips with our lives and accept realities that have hindered our growth. We are passing through something that will liberate us or perhaps enslave us.

So pace yourself, savor the moments. Too often, nerves can set in and sabotage a performance. After all, moments are all you have. Singers have music. Artists have brush strokes. The actor has to take the time to relish life's odd, funny, serious, and sad experiences. Don't cheat yourself or an audience. Time is on your side and it is your greatest ally.

HOME ACTING PLAYBOOK

1. Select a simple nursery rhyme. Play around doing it in different styles. For example, try it like a serious drama, a romantic comedy, or a sci-fi thriller. Refer to the appendix for Websites listing more genres to explore.

2. Take a monologue that is isolated from a whole script. You can select one from the appendix for example. Come up with five different events or moments before that preceded the script. See how different scenarios modify the way you deliver your speech.

3. Describe an important event that happened to you recently as if you have to share it with a friend for a crucial reason. For example, you might tell a lawyer friend about a crime. Or you might tell a best friend about a car accident. Next, do the same story again in two contrasting styles. Say it once in the style of a romantic comedy and then say it with a film noir feel or any style you know.

STUDY THE STARS

▸ Favorite Sports Character: Cuba Gooding Jr. in *Jerry Maguire*
▸ Classic Western Character: Alan Ladd in *Shane*
▸ Great Criminal Personas: Robert Mitchum in *Cape Fear* and Charlize Theron in *Monster*

▶ Media Resources: Review AFI movie listings in the appendix and look at current films for emerging trends. Watch a few minutes of episodes from a sitcom, detective show, and reality show and compare the acting styles (reality TV has casting calls, so don't be fooled by the documentary style).

7

Inspiration, Research, and Imagination

Actors may find period pieces difficult to tackle. They may feel hampered by the language or unconnected to the material. Creative research, however, can inspire ideas and ignite the imagination to help you transcend different eras. Every tangible detail you uncover can enable you to immerse yourself in a role. Consider how Mozart and Elvis Presley reflected the collective mood of their times. Music can set the tempo for your character's world.

Digging into the details about every facet of daily life is important. You may want to explore a workplace environment, or you may be curious about the clothing worn for a particular part. Explore leisure time activities in relation to social class as you shape your role.

Your probing may be more psychological as well. Sometimes, you will play a disturbed person and you will want to understand the driving force behind the psychosis or neurosis. You'll then figure out how to internalize and externalize the traits for your character. Inspiration for this may come from watching people in different settings. Unfortunately, today we have many homeless people to use for a variety of extreme characters, and these people are very visible.

Observing a range of people in different settings is often helpful. You can also watch animals for insights into movement and temperament. I have, for instance, a very clear picture of the three cunning lionesses from the movie *Earth* narrated by James Earl Jones. The fierce eyes of these animals watching for prey as they drink water speak volumes.

There are also volumes of books for historical reference as you begin to work on a part. Museums display artifacts from everyday life. Paintings and sculpture show us artistic interpretations of a culture. Impressionist art, for example, portrays a muted version of life. These pictures are romantic and not representational, whereas Edward Hopper's *Nighthawks* creates a real and stark version of the world. The simplest artifacts from the mundane world such as spears and spoons can also help you imagine how your character lived. The Internet offers a vast treasure trove of video, pictures, and information on all of the aforementioned research ideas. Refer to the appendix for suggested Websites.

Costumes enable us to think about personal movement. You can observe where the body is restricted or free to move about. High collars, for instance, would hamper neck movement. You can also explore different senses for inspiration. Ask yourself, what did the fabric feel like? What were the scents in the room? How did the furniture feel? Was it stiff or soft? What sounds were present?

Of course, economic factors come into play too. You need to consider the overall social strata of the culture. Envision the comfortable lifestyle of a middle-class American family in the 1950s. In contrast, imagine how a middle-class family of the Great Depression would be stripped of all their comforts and have to scramble for mere necessities.

Politics can also pose challenges for a character both globally and personally. When the world is at a critical war, the stakes in life will be higher than during a booming peacetime. Different personality types in a workplace or social setting will also determine specific acting choices. A loud pushy boss may make a timid uptight male employee miserable at an office, for example.

Spatial factors are so important to consider. Are the surroundings shabby or lavish? Imagine wearing a stuffy suit in a California office without air-conditioning in the 1880s, or that you are dressed in finery at a swanky party with caviar in the 1920s.

By defining concrete scene elements, you can begin to visualize any period. This gets your imagination flowing so that you can establish your personal physical space. You'll consider what food you would eat and the manner you would consume it. For instance, think of the clichéd medieval scenes where large pieces of meat are consumed sloppily. In contrast, imagine the dainty manners of the old South portrayed in *Gone with the Wind*. When I studied at HB Studio, I was encouraged to acquire *The Timetables of History,* which is listed in the suggested reading section. This book plots out the politics, art, music, literature, and inventions of different eras.

ADD DEPTH TO YOUR ROLE

The more layers you can add to your role, the more fleshed out it will be for you. Beyond that, be a good translator. Observe real scenes in your world and imagine what they would be like in a different era. Inspiration comes from a creatively fertile mind. Music, art, life, and walks in the park can free your thoughts to wander and make new connections and associations. Sometimes when I've worked exhaustively on a part, I go to a museum the day before the performance to relax and take in the artistic stimulations. New ideas ignite the imagination. Exercise can also help you make uninhibited connections to your part.

Research is like gathering pieces of a puzzle. You then use your imagination and put the pieces together. It engages you to create new interpretations of your material. Don't forget to study the language of your monologue or scene in the context of its time period too. Improvise an everyday conversation—take an hour and sporadically play with moments that would be in your character's day.

Endow objects in your home with qualities in your scene. Make it very detailed. If you can draw, sketch out everything that would complete your space. Today there is no excuse not to do research with the embarrassment of riches on the Internet. You can see videos of people on YouTube. Search engines can give you an array of pictures of art, costumes, and weaponry from different times and places. The more you know, the more you'll be inspired to fulfill your character's course of action and truly imagine that you are living and breathing in the moment for your monologue or audition scene.

HIDDEN TREASURES

Digging deeper, you might find untapped resources as you begin to take on a role. Be inventive and tailor the part from raw materials you have and the mundane elements that may be in your character's life. Learn to think like your character by solving simple everyday problems.

For example, how would you fix something that is broken? We have all had to come up with alternative methods to repair something. Consider how your character goes about mending broken items. What kinds of thought processes are employed? Insight and inventiveness emerge from necessity. People who are good problem solvers may be less troubled by new adjustments in life. Perhaps the opposite is true too. For example, your character can't change a light-bulb and may get upset with little things that go wrong.

Do a timeline for your character. What is a typical morning like? Think of holidays, normal days, and times of crisis too. Chart out a day, week, and year to get a sense of the mundane and extraordinary events that occur.

Also consider how your character reacts to different emotional triggers that transpire in situations. We have so many thoughts that are hidden in our mind that may not be apparent under normal circumstances. A childhood trauma is suppressed so that we can go about our normal activities and function. However, a critical event can set off the feelings of fear and foreboding that lie buried. In essence, a secret is revealed.

Many emotions lay dormant and ready to surface whenever a trigger sets them off. The depth of your character's passions can be hidden until an event illuminates them. We are constantly subverting thoughts in our everyday life to function "normally." Do an internal monologue for your character consisting of random thoughts. Experiment and see what happens. No matter what, a range of unplanned thoughts and emotions can pop up for your character based on situations and actions in a scene. Use the feelings of shame, delight, or angst that may emerge as you rehearse parts to add new dimensions to your performances.

Feeding your imagination and staying playful can be an important tool as you prepare for last-minute auditions and cold reads. If you can just remember that you're simply engaging in make-believe activities, you might actually have fun. Practicing ahead of time can help you make choices faster. Here are some simple guidelines to help keep your creative juices flowing even when you have little prep time and may have to do a cold read.

FAST TRACK CHECKLIST

Consult this simple checklist to make quick decisions if you have little preparation time. Also remember the basic improvisation breakdown of the *who, what*, and *where* elements of the scene if you have even less time. Define who you are, what you are doing, and where you are. Determine what the story is about. Otherwise, you can delve as deeply as time permits to devise more choices. Experiment with these shortcuts on your own with scripts so that you can start to make faster choices. If you don't practice, it will take longer to figure things out on auditions and you may become more nervous. Home workouts can help you gain more confidence and hopefully keep you relaxed so you can be creative too.

Pretend Parameters

First decide: how close is this character to you? For example, if you're auditioning for a real person commercial character, you might imagine that you are simply talking to a friend you know to keep your performance natural. On the other hand, if your character is farther from who you are, you may have to add physical traits or perhaps an accent to play a broader type. Once you have your pretend parameters figured out, then you can focus on other factors.

Body

Make some choices to engage your body both externally and internally. Visualize your physical space around you and imagine how your body feels. Establish the place and your relation to it with all the clues that you're given in the script. Think about your immediate physical space—What might you wear? Are you hungry, thirsty, drunk, or cold? What time is it? Is the environment friendly, familiar, or frightening? In short, define your physical comfort level.

Logic

Define the logical course of actions for you in the scene. What has just happened? What do you want to happen? Draw on any improvisation experience to think about how you would proceed in a scene like yours. For example, if your friend was just murdered, you might seek revenge or justice.

Heart

Figure out what you want most from the scene and your partner. What are you willing to fight for? How important is it to you? Are you rational, dispassionate, out of control, or calm? Make some choices about the people and things you care about and consider how your inner feelings determine your actions.

Mind

Decide what you think about your life, the situation, and your scene partner. This can be your hidden agenda where your secrets lie and it can be a powerful tool to help you get off the words. If time permits, do a quick internal monologue about the scene.

History

Focus on how your past colors the present situation. For example, have you always been a loser, but this is your one shot to change your life? Pick some key moments from your past that might play into this scene. You won't have time for a backstory but at least you can add another layer to your role.

HOME ACTING PLAYBOOK

1. Imagine your character is in his therapist's office. Make specific choices about the therapist, your relationship, and the office. Express your character's current concerns in a monologue. Will your character need more sessions? What information is not revealed?

2. Find something that needs to be fixed and try to mend it. Do it as your character would do it. Perform any routine activity. Get dressed, clean the house, or make coffee as your character. Then do your monologue or rehearse a scene while you do the activity.

3. Take a simple bit of advertising copy from a magazine. Imagine that you are doing it as if you are (1) in prehistoric times, (2) the Renaissance, and (3) the Roaring Twenties. Now do some research about these eras and think about the lifestyles of the people and repeat the exercise.

4. Here's a variation on the classic improv game called *Object Transformation*. Take an ordinary object like a pen, ball, or Kleenex and use it while doing the time travel exercise in the aforementioned practice, but imagine that it is a historically accurate prop for your scene.

Explore different uses for your object as you improvise various scenes.

5. Pick three of your favorite characters from movies, plays, or literature. Go to your closet and select a piece of wardrobe that best matches your character's essence. Wear it and do an improvisation of the character in everyday life.

6. Select a soliloquy such as Hamlet's "To be or not to be" or Joan of Arc's speech near the very end of Shaw's *St. Joan* beginning with the line, "Yes, they told me you were fools." Read it over and say it to your imagined scene partner. Record it if you can. Next think about a real scene from your life now. What events would motivate you to say these things and to whom would you tell it? Create an improvised monologue of your speech. Record it if you can.

Now, go back to your original speech and do it right away. Record it if you can and compare your three performances.

7. In yoga, there is a mirror exercise in which you imagine seeing yourself fifteen years ago, now, and fifteen years in the future. Gaze at yourself in a real mirror and imagine what you would look like as a king or queen or a poverty-stricken person throughout different times in history. Now turn your back on the mirror and see the fourth wall for the characters that you just saw in the mirror. Finally, let your mind be free and fluid and just imagine you are in the space of that period. See the details of the space and move about.

8. Observe your surroundings when you go out of your house. Then imagine people are moving in the same place in a different time period. Think about how these people would be dressed and what sounds you would hear.

9. Watch movies and documentaries depicting a range of places and times throughout history. Create a character you might play in one of these scenarios and do an improvised monologue.

Work on personal soliloquies. This draws on the clichéd monologue we all do when we express what we will say to someone about a pressing issue. For instance, we rehearse out loud what we might say to a boss when we want to ask for a raise. Refer to Kevin Costner's scenes in which he is rehearsing his introduction to James Earl Jones's character in *Field of Dreams* for an example. Come up with three of these kinds of speeches for yourself and, if you can, record them and observe your performance.

STUDY THE STARS

▶ Classic Time Period Movies: *Gladiator, Pride & Prejudice, Gone with the Wind, 2001: A Space Odyssey*

▶ Roles Stretching an Actor's Imagination: *The Curious Case of Benjamin Button, Being John Malkovich*

▶ Media Resources: http://www.history.com/. Do a search of Shakespeare on the Web for resources, videos, and films. Visit a local history museum or search for specific historical pictures online (refer to a site that is listed in the appendix).

▶ Study art styles and music through different ages. Beef up your imagination and create puppet characters that time travel. Use historical Websites to learn more about your eras.

8

Practical Tips for Auditions and Performances

You constantly have to find ways to practice your craft, whether you are paid for your efforts or not. Juggling a survival job with everything else can be tricky, so it's good to be organized. Hopefully you'll find flexible work and an understanding boss who will support your erratic schedule. Being prepared to perform can help ease your tensions.

The audition process should be fun in spite of all your other obligations. Nonetheless, you'll have a lot of details to take care of prior to your performance. So I've created a checklist to help you approach your unique situation. Here are some key elements to address: time, text, creative choices, preparation, and performance.

TIME

First, you must consider the amount of time you have to prepare for a part and the size of your role. If you have an audition of a three-page monologue to deliver within a day, then you will have to work diligently to prepare the part. On the other hand, if you have a single-line audition due at the end of the week, you can play around with it and relax a bit. However, remember that a single line requires a lot of creative thought. You must jump into a scene with as much energy as the other actors in the scenario.

All parts have specific requirements and you must know how to approach each role. As you become more experienced, you'll learn that sheer practice and rehearsal may be necessary for a longer part, while a lot of imaginative work comes into play for shorter roles. Either way, the time constraints will dictate your game plan. If you work in television, you may have rewrites on the set the day your scene is shot. This creates an urgency that may, in fact, help you pick up your lines quickly. On the other hand, if you have a full week to prepare for an audition, you'll have a chance to reflect on your choices. You can also take the time to go into great detail about your character's traits, the scene, and detecting the clues in the script.

You want to fully study the text no matter how big your part is. Read it over several times before you rehearse it out loud, if possible. Resist the temptation to learn your part too early and establish rote patterns. Determine the given facts in the script and either write them down or think about them. We all have different styles of learning. Use what mode suits you best. Glean every known detail that the author gives you for your scene. Get a sense of who your character is and where the scene takes place. Decide what your objectives are. Envision your pre-life, the setting, and your wardrobe.

Then take a break and put the script down. Do some routine physical activity to let the facts sink in and give your brain a rest. When you go back to the script, make some specific choices for your dialogue. Ponder what is beneath the words. When time is limited, some actors will do a quick list of emotions for each line. For example, you write words like *anger*, *love*, or *fear* next to the lines. Although you want to resist the temptation to learn your role too early and get locked into patterns, you can still say the lines out loud with different emotions for each line. This can help you create variety and become familiar with the words so that you can pick them up easily in the audition if you don't have time to memorize the text. Hopefully, you can go beyond this checklist and dig deeper and not have to rely only on cues. Either way, you'll need to fully understand your character's motivations in the scene.

If your part is large, try to improvise it and say what is really on your character's mind so that you understand why you are saying your dialogue. Conversely, if your part is small, you may want to embellish the moments surrounding the scene. Improvise other scenes with characters to establish relationships and connections. Say your internal dialogue out loud as you rehearse your scene. To practice, you can record your cue lines and then leave spaces for your lines of dialogue. Focus on your internal monologue as you play the tape.

Relax and Focus

Once again, don't forget to take a break. Meditative work that you learn in yoga classes can be useful to free up new thoughts. Lie on your back and progressively let your body relax. Breathe and focus on a neutral word such as *om* or *love*. Think about your character's life. Try to imagine everyday scenes. Let any thoughts flow freely. Establishing a tangible setting can be useful in an audition because it will be there to help you stay focused. Finally, just relax and breathe.

You may find it helpful to take a walk or get on a stationary bike and try to forget everything. Perhaps you'll want to review your script instead. Walking helps get both sides of the brain working. Go over your part and let the freedom of your movements feed your creative process. Exercise or physical activities can be helpful while you go over lines because you can get off the words and vary your choices. I will often tidy up the house and recite my dialogue. Juggling is wonderful to do while playing with lines. Don't lock yourself into repetitive patterns, stay fluid and keep exploring new angles for the character.

Once more, take a break and relax. Give your brain a rest while you organize all of your thoughts. If you have pages to say and feel overwhelmed, then go over your part right before you go to bed. Play the audition tape you have created. When you go back to the text and rehearse it, put down the script and perform it as a mime scene. Get a sense of the pure physical life of your character. Also, experiment with an opposite genre. If it's a drama, laugh while you do it. If it's a comedy, be sad. Take it way out of its normal zone to find new colors. Do it in accents or gibberish and then go back to your rehearsal process.

Also personalize the role and find strong connections to your life that help make it real. Write *as if* equivalents next to each line that connect you to the character. For example, I'll write, "It's as if my son was expelled from school," next to a line. Figure out how your character is like people you know. Do the same for any other scene partners you might interact with in the script. Find similar overriding themes and objectives in your own life that match the scene.

On the day of the audition, don't panic if you can't remember your lines. You'll have the script in your hand and you can pick up dialogue as needed. In fact, you should hold the script so that you don't seem like you are presenting a final performance. You never know when you might drop a line.

In some instances, you may have to do a cold read. How can you prepare for this situation? Never underestimate the power of practicing the process consistently. Voice-over is a quick study medium, as is improvisation. Rehearse constantly so that you are ready to take on roles. You can't get rusty. You must be disciplined enough to practice doing cold reads, learning parts, and performing regularly so that you are ready for anything. Work with a friend on scenes if you can't afford a class.

It is a good idea to rehearse doing scripts ice-cold, where you have to pick up the lines off the page and look up to deliver the words. The goal is to learn to look at a line and take the time to remember it and deliver it to camera. Practice this technique for those auditions when there is very little prep time. Acquire scripts and analyze them on the spot and make fast choices. Then, rehearse or record a pretend audition. The goal in all of your auditions will be to get off the page and play to camera the best you can. So even if you can't memorize a script, learn how to maximize your time on camera.

You don't want to miss out on a great opportunity because you are simply too lazy to work at your craft. Downtime is often when I work out the most. The industry may be slow, but I know that I must be ready to perform at a professional level at any time so I don't rest. If you practice consistently, then you'll be prepared for a long or short role, no matter what kind of turnaround time you may have.

TEXT

In the beginning, all you have to work with are the writer's words. The style of writing, the depth of the piece, and the directions you are given will dictate your creative strategies. For example, Shakespeare may be dense and difficult if you have never studied his work. On the other hand, a small part from a sitcom may seem simple and easy. Both scripts pose unique challenges. The more you become familiar with different styles of writing, the easier it will be to understand how to approach the material. Therefore, you should study classical and contemporary plays as well as TV and film scripts. If you are auditioning for commercials, then you'll want to become more versed in that copy too.

Today there is no excuse for you not to rehearse a range of parts. You can use the Internet to research everything from plays to monologues. However, you may have to pay fees to download current TV and film scripts on sites like showfax.com. You can always work with a friend and transcribe scripts from film and TV. This way, you won't watch the performance and be tempted to copy it. No matter what your goals are, your homework will pay off.

I always say in voice-over to raise the bar. So if you've never read a classical play or worked on a large part, you should do it. Hopefully, you'll have some sense of what you are best suited to perform and concentrate your energy there. Nonetheless, if you tackle more difficult material on your own, then you may find it easier to do lighter scripts. It's similar to the idea that you study opera or ballet if you want to sing or dance. Aim for something higher in your workouts so that you can come into auditions with confidence.

When you're given an audition script, you need to categorize it first. Decide what genre it is, figure out if it is film or TV, and define your purpose in the scene. For example, you may be intended to be a suspicious character in a murder mystery. On the other hand, you may just be passing through the scene if you are dropping off a phone message to a boss, so don't overact ever. Consider what the audience wants to see from your character. Imagine you are watching this scene and figure out what you would expect. You also want to know the style of the show or film. If you are doing a part for a recurring episode, then you'll want to watch the show. In fact, you should be watching shows, films, plays, or commercials that are relevant to your audition scripts. Be prepared and study performances in the marketplace.

In addition, you need to scrutinize the writer's style. Let the flow of the language help you craft your part. Character and scene descriptions will also give you more crucial clues so read them thoroughly. You must use every piece of evidence you have if you only have sides for your audition and then fill in pertinent missing information with your imagination. Sometimes you must make educated guesses, while in other instances, you'll be given a lot of concrete information to help you play your part.

In both instances, you need to find the emotional life beneath the text. A character has strong wants or needs whether he speaks with an upper-crust tone or lower-class slang. The language does tell you so much about your social class and situation. Take whatever information you are given and embellish it to create a unique role that is faithful to the text and believable for the scene.

CREATIVE CHOICES

The choices you make about your characterization are first dictated by the information in the script, but then you add your own individual interpretation to the part. Review the many roles that Meryl Streep has brought to life. She makes believable choices that add a richness and depth to each character.

In essence, an actor has endless choices to make when crafting a role. The details can be shaped by the genre, script style, and the amount of preparation time prior to the performance. If you have ever seen Hollywood screen tests, then you can observe the different ways actors approach the same part. Certainly performers are suited to some characters rather than others, but the individual choices have great impact.

For example, Mickey Rourke used a very raw, rugged, and poignant approach to his interpretation of *The Wrestler*. These choices were appropriate. On the other hand, Julia Roberts's silly antics in *Pretty Woman* evoke a great deal of pathos. Beneath this glossy finish, an actor lays so much groundwork that the audience never sees. Perhaps a rich pre-life or backstory helps to paint a painful life. Sometimes strong sense memory work can bring realistic moments to a scene. The setting or place may be endowed with strong emotions to create an authentic world for the performer to create credible work. Every part dictates different paths. An actor must experiment and find the best methods to spark his imagination and believe he is a living and breathing human in a specific circumstance.

Your work can be more interesting if you make very specific choices. Generalizations often are clichéd. For example, if I'm playing a mobster, I can be tempted to simply play a thug. However, if you take the time to examine the life that led up to this line of work, you may find fresh insights. By breaking down every element in the scene specifically, you can make it more realistic. Paul Sills stressed the importance of specificity in acting when I took his class. He used the example that it's not a ring—it's a pinky ring with an emerald and three diamonds.

In theater, a role can grow with each performance. New insights and revelations will emerge on a nightly basis. An on-camera actor must analyze a script well and lay a strong foundation for a part. A lot of preparation must be done prior to shooting, so it's important to find a method that works best for you. Perhaps you can find someone to help you run lines. As stated before, I've recorded a tape with the other actor's dialogue and left a space for me to say my lines.

PREPARATION

Preparation can mean many things to a performer. There is the journey an actor takes to learn the craft of acting. Then there is a rehearsal process the performer uses to prepare for a role. Finally, there are the preparatory moments before an actor goes on stage or before the camera.

Of course, time is everything. How much experience you have will determine the difficulty of roles you can master. The amount of time you have to lay the foundation for your performance will dictate the depth of your interpretation. Your actual performance will be tempered by your ability to catapult yourself into the character full throttle. As you become more proficient, you will learn shortcuts to breaking down scenes, selecting wardrobe for auditions, and getting the feel for a part. The process will be streamlined.

A novice will learn from mistakes with each audition. It can help to break down the tasks into crucial components: (1) read and analyze the part, (2) decide what wardrobe may be needed, (3) make choices about your character and experiment in the rehearsal process for the best ways to play the role, (4) learn the part and polish it. No matter what, don't feel pressured. You need to be creative and playful as you work on the script. Your wardrobe can suggest your character, unless you are given specific instructions on what to wear, such as for a commercial audition.

Preparing to perform is the icing on the cake. This is your time and you deserve it. Too often, actors can sabotage their efforts with negative thoughts. This is inappropriate prior to a performance. The best plan is to focus on your character's compelling desires. Don't let anything stand in the way of your ability to quiet down and focus before an audition or performance. Give yourself plenty of time to drive and park before your audition appointment. Think about your overriding objective as you wait in the lobby or with other actors backstage prior to going on stage. Don't be distracted by actor chatter. After all, you should allow yourself the luxury to do your best.

PERFORMANCE

When you arrive at an audition, be pleasant, but try to keep your task in mind. Review your character's needs. Simply greet the casting director and think real thoughts about the scene you will be in. Relive the moment before the scene happens. Endow the space you are in with tangible elements from your character's world. Feel the things that are logical to the scene, hear the sounds, slow down, and breathe. Then allow yourself the time to work moment to moment.

Even if you don't feel fully prepared, don't panic. Give way to the make-believe world. If you are given a script at the last minute, allow yourself room for error, but don't lose focus on being in the scene. Enjoy the process. Don't put pressure on yourself to book the job at an audition. Be free and play. React to new unexpected twists and turns. Above all, turn off censors in your head and find ways to pull yourself back into the imaginary world of the scenario.

Everybody wants you to succeed. In fact, casting directors, and producers need you to do well. Help them out. Be a strong, self-assured performer. Casting directors don't work if they can't bring in good performers. Producers lose money if they don't have strong actors. Audiences don't get the much-needed diversion from their everyday lives if you don't entertain them. So know how important you are and don't fall into the trap of feeling unworthy. As I said in my voice-over book, think of yourself as the hero ready to save the day, and not a doormat actor ready to be stepped on.

Finally, breathe and smile when you are done and thank the casting director. If you feel you did poorly, keep a notebook and write all your thoughts down quickly and then forget it. You can review your notes at a later time if you feel you need to revisit something. Otherwise, move on. Save your energy because you'll need to be fresh for your next exciting venture.

AUDITION TIPS AT A GLANCE

- Do deep breathing when you arrive.
- Pinpoint tension in your body and release it.
- React to everything like your character would.
- Turn down the actor chatter in the lobby and turn up your character's interior monologue.
- Celebrate your chance to perform, no matter what obstacles you face.
- See casting professionals as your allies.
- Be strong and assured, not wimpy and whiny.
- Never ask questions that are answered in your script or posted outside the casting office.
- Be pleasant and professional, but not overly chatty in the audition.
- Remember that last-minute directions can help you to be spontaneous.

9

Expert Advice from Industry Insiders

I've given you an overview of script analysis, acting techniques, and basic rules for performing in different situations. Now find out what a range of industry experts has to say about their expectations for professional actors in this chapter. It's important to learn from other performers' mistakes to plot a successful career course. So use these interviews to help you avoid pitfalls that hinder your progress.

WHY IS A MONOLOGUE IMPORTANT?

Selena Smith is a regional SAG-AFTRA-EQUITY (S-A-E) agent who has worked with many actors through the years. She sums up why a monologue is an indispensable tool for an actor.

"The monologue has been the actor's lifeline since the age of Elizabethan actors. It is a live resume, a sample of an actor's work. . . . Every actor needs a staple of no less than ten sets of monologues that can compare and contrast their skill set. As an agent, the monologue is the best tool to see a complete character in a performance-ready environment.

"More often than not, a bad monologue will end an audition of any kind."

The monologue is also an important device for the writer to convey information. John Truby is a top Hollywood story consultant and the author of *The Anatomy of Story: 22 Steps to Becoming a Master Storyteller.* He describes how the monologue works within a story.

"The classic use of monologue is to express the mind of the character, to get into the interior of the character. That, of course, is much more common in theater than in film. A monologue is also useful if the character needs to give a speech that expresses their deepest values in some way. You use a monologue to give the schtick of the character, whatever their trademark approach or style. For example, in comedy, the monologue is also classically used to make a confession, and it's used when a character wants to make a moral argument to justify what they've done."

Truby also discusses how this performance piece is useful to evaluate an actor's talent.

"A monologue is a story in miniature. So the director or producer may want to see if the actor can craft a full emotional journey over the course of a story: in this case, a miniature version of a story. [They] might want to see if the actor can own the stage. And of course they'll use a monologue to see if the actor can find the meaning in the words because you don't have another actor to play off of. So it's a . . . different level of talent to be able to make a monologue work."

MONOLOGUES FOR AGENTS AND AUDITIONS

New York agent Sue Winik of Sheplin-Winik Artists represents film, TV, and theater actors. She gives practical insights about why monologues are important in the industry.

"Monologues are used today in the general audition. It will not get you a job. It gives the casting person an idea of who you are—your technique/training—sense of self—and if you have the skills to perform in their production. Monologues are used more in the theater genre but may also be used in film/TV. More important than talent, it gives us an idea of who you are as a person and do we want to work with you."

Although every agent is different, Sue Winik wants actors to perform monologues.

"I like to hear monologues in my office so I can see that an actor knows how to prepare. I like to talk a lot to the actor to know them as people so I get a sense of who they are and where they fit in with the people I like to represent. . . . Inappropriate material is always a turn off for me. With all the material in the world to choose from, there is no reason for inappropriate material to be used. This choice does indeed tell me something about the actor. Sometimes more than they want me to know."

Most actors are always looking for the perfect monologue. Here are some tips Sue Winik shares that may help you pick the appropriate piece.

"In selecting a monologue, choose one that fits who you are as a person. That you strongly connect with as a person. It needs to be appropriate (*please*!). All monologues should be under two minutes—that means—*one minute forty-five seconds tops*. Have your coach stopwatch it. This gives you time to breathe. An actor should know that a director decides in the first fifteen seconds if this actor is right for a callback. These things are based on type, can we understand your diction, do you give off good vibes and do we want to work with you, or do you have attitude and appear difficult to work with. *Fifteen seconds*. The rest is gratis time for the actor.

"An actor should stick to the genre in which he is most comfortable and knowledgeable. If you are classically trained and want to do the classics—pick pieces that are appropriate to your age and type. Don't be limited to Shakespeare. Molière and Goldsmith, Shaw, etc., [are] also acceptable. Choose material that is *not* heard every day. How many Romeos/Petruchios/Juliets can a director stand in one day?

"If you are a contemporary actor, do what you do best of drama/comedy. Don't pick anything over the top. Any histrionics/bad language will more likely turn off a director and maybe even scare him off. I had an actor (who did get the job, by the way) who did some over-the-top things at an audition and had a "special" callback with the director so the director could make sure the actor wasn't really 'crazy.' The actor was not crazy—just a little *too* over-the-top creative."

Every audition will have its own unique parameters so you will have to modify your monologue to meet the needs of the specific medium and casting situation. Sue Winik also offers great advice about adapting your material to different situations.

"In film, if a monologue is put on tape, acting is all in the eyes. Are you believable? The focus is truly on the other person and what we feel and want from him. Any introspection on lines kills this."

WHAT ARE THE COMMON TRAITS OF SUCCESSFUL AUDITIONS?

As sides or cold reads are used more frequently to audition actors, it's good to learn how experts evaluate performances. Actors who are unprepared often lose parts. Successful actors do their homework and can take direction well. The following interviews reveal how many performers are unable to meet the professional standards necessary to win parts. As you read this section, evaluate how you approach auditions and try to establish better habits.

Craig Campobasso is a Los Angeles casting director. He was nominated for an Emmy® for his casting in David E. Kelley's *Picket Fences*. He started out in the business as an actor, so he also understands the process. He shares insights on how to create professional auditions.

"How does an actor achieve getting into the 10% of actors that make it to callbacks? By being prepared. Reading the script. Research who the director is [and] break down your character. Making strong choices for the audition scenes. Go to a professional acting coach who can help you determine your choices, and show you the symbology in a scene that pertains to the character.

"When at the audition, listen to the direction being given to you. If you are given three notes and you only take one note in the redirect, you have most likely lost the role. Most actors will do it the same way, even though they were given clear and precise direction. If this is the case with you, go to an on-camera class, so that when you are being directed by your acting coach, you can watch the video and see how much you remembered of the direction and if you took [it] appropriately.

"To memorize a scene, handwrite the exposition in black, your character in red and the other character in blue. It will give your mind a visual remembrance of the words and action. Or you can talk the scene into a tape recorder and listen to it over and over. Note—in an audition, always hold your sides. Never lay them on the table or don't bring them in because you're trying to impress us with your memorizing skills. We want you to impress us with your acting skills. Yes, we want to have it memorized, but holding them will ensure a smooth and seamless audition, as you can refer to them if you forget a line.

"Another trick for learning to remember emotion and lines is to highlight each emotion in a different color. For example, if you have a chunk of dialogue and the first paragraph is anger, highlight in orange. If the second paragraph is resentment, highlight in yellow. If the third paragraph is remorse, highlight in blue. Write the 'emotion' next to the color bar . . .

"[A] great quick audition technique is a Meisner technique: doable actions. It's where you assign a line of dialogue an action or a verb. It's a quick way to grasp the emotional state of the character and hook into their feeling . . . so the performance is natural."

Caroline Sinclair is a New York City casting director for films, theater, commercials, and music videos. Since she sees such a wide array of actors, you can apply her knowledge to your favorite form of acting. She talks about how actors impress her most.

"For me, the most important skill that successful actors demonstrate is the art of listening. I love it when actors come into the room and make a choice, even if that choice is wrong, and then when you give them an adjustment, they do it perfectly. That is so exciting. And it shows that they listen and understand the material."

STRATEGIES FOR THEATER AND WEBISODE AUDITIONS

Television has unique demands and so does theater. Dan Leslie is a member of the Artistic Committee at Theatre 40 in Beverly Hills and he offers helpful tips about auditions. First, he talks about what kind of material is used for auditions.

"Actors are required to prepare two contrasting monologues—one classical and one contemporary. Our play selections for the season run the gamut as far as style and time periods are concerned. We need actors who can handle heightened language as well as everyday speech."

Dan Leslie says that each monologue is limited to three minutes when a large number of performers are seen in one day. Next he discusses how actors succeed in auditions.

"They have done their homework. They have obviously thought about their pieces and the characters within them. Good actors understand *variety*. Their monologues have changes in volume and pace. Dramatic monologues have humor and funny monologues have serious parts. Look for material that they haven't seen before. Ladies: avoid Viola's ring speech from *Twelfth Night*.

"Occasionally, we will ask an actor to repeat a monologue and give them a nonsensical adjustment. (Do it like a standup comic, for example). Good actors just go with this and often come up with wonderful new shadings.

"For Theatre 40 specifically: we are looking not only for good actors, but that rare actor who wants to assist us in running the company. Think about the aspects of play production that you are interested in/have an aptitude for."

Dan Leslie also shares his insights into how performers impress producers with acting sides when they are auditioning within the company.

"The words come off the page. They bring nuance and ideas to the scene. When the director gives them an adjustment, they can truly take it in and change their performance, not repeat what they did before. Technically, they keep their script low and away from their face."

Brian Gramo is a director and Web entrepreneur who founded the live interactive television network theStream.tv. Brian has worked with actors on scripted webisodes. He shares insights into how performers can impress directors on auditions.

"When it comes to casting webisodes, you have to understand that you're working at a much lower, lower budget level than some other productions, so you're going to look for someone that is a team player in more ways than one. You know, perhaps you didn't have enough time to write, so maybe if they're good improvisers, they're going to have an advantage over someone that just knows how to memorize a script and deliver the lines."

WHAT DO ACTORS DO WRONG IN AUDITIONS?

Actors don't get parts for a variety of reasons. Dan Leslie delineates flaws with auditions he casts at Theatre 40.

"The big mistakes usually come in the classical (i.e., Shakespeare) monologues. The actors have not 'decoded' the Elizabethan verse for themselves, and so they can't convey the meaning to *us*. They recite the words with nothing behind them. Also some simple technical stuff: placing their invisible partner to the side of them so they turn away from us, dropping their volume at the ends of sentences, etc. Also, and you'd think this would be a no-brainer—*bring the social skills*. Don't get furious when someone asks you the titles of your pieces (yeah, it happened to me once)."

Dan Leslie also talks about how performers lose parts within the company.

"The mistakes come when you totally concentrate on the words. Your face never leaves the script and we don't get to see what you think and feel. When you are putting meaning and emotion behind the words, nobody is going to care if you occasionally lose your place. Don't be afraid to ask about words or moments that you don't understand. You can look bad if you mispronounce [a] character's name or an important place."

Brian Gramo also talks about how actors cling to the words and don't sound natural for the webisodes he casts.

"I think a lot of actors mess up in auditions. They're so concerned about, I guess, being understood and saying the words exactly and properly that they are over enunciating and then they start to sound fake. And I try to describe to them I'm like 'Hey, if you're talking to your friends, you're gonna slur a little bit, you're going to use contractions, you're going to have your accent.' And so this person has to live in that real world too. They're not, you know, they're not reading the instructions for something, . . . You need to speak normally and . . . hopefully if it's memorized, you need to be able to read the lines, or at least read off the page naturally."

Be Prepared and Professional

Caroline Sinclair addresses the issues she finds troubling with actors in auditions.

"I feel that some of the biggest mistakes actors make when coming to auditions are firstly not being prepared. I feel that if the actor has not been given a reasonable time with the material, he or she should always try and reschedule. Sometimes clearly that is not an option, but when it is offered, one should definitely take it. One cannot always be off-book, but I feel that it is really frustrating when the actor barely looks up and you cannot see their eyes. The eyes are, after all, the key to the soul and to the camera. Another mistake that inexperienced actors will do in film auditions is paying no mind to the camera and wandering all over the place. I cannot stress enough the importance of learning about the camera.

"Also, another problem is not relating to the reader but doing it straight to camera. That is really a basic mistake but I have seen many young and starting out actors doing it. The final mistake for me is when people come into the room and they are chatting about everything under the sun rather than the job at hand. Inevitably, they are not focused on the material and their audition will suffer. Be friendly after the audition, but do the work first."

Craig Campobasso concurs that many actors come unprepared to auditions. He adds these insights.

"If an actor is reading for a lead role, they must go in-depth into the character to study behavior in each audition scene. They must read the script. Find three different choices of preparing the scene, then make a strong choice. When the casting director or director gives you more direction, then you will have already rehearsed it the other ways, giving you an advantage over other auditioners."

Campobasso also describes how performers sabotage their best efforts: "Actors [who] come in and say that they just got the sides, when they've had days to prepare. So what they really are saying is that they don't take acting seriously and are telling the casting director that they won't do well in the audition. If you were the casting director, would you consider them for the role?

"Actors/Actresses who wear cologne or perfume. That's a big no-no. We're stuck in those cubicles of an office all day, and with all those scents going on, we get sinus headaches."

Campobasso says that actors who talk incessantly can "talk themselves out of the role. So when a decision is being made with the casting director and director on certain choices, we will always choose the professional actor over the talker."

Agent Sue Winik also lists below some obvious but relevant mistakes many actors make:

- Not being prepared
- Read play, if available
- Work with coach
- Know lines, don't wing it!
- Bad attitude
- Dressing inappropriately—not necessarily as the character would dress.
- Hygiene
- Choosing the wrong material

- Over the top
- Incorrect genre
- *Arriving late*!! (Sooooooo unprofessional!)
- Making apologies and excuses for not being prepared/ on time, etc.
- Pix and resumes not attached

Making Adjustments and Working Within a Time Frame

Every medium has its own rules and expectations. The amount of turnaround depends on production schedules and timing. You never know when you might hear of something last-minute. Craig Campobasso discusses how film and TV auditions are often scheduled.

"Most actors have the material twenty-four hours or more before an audition. Cold reading is to show us your acting skills in a short period of rehearsal time to see if you have a grasp of the character's state of mind. TV auditions are fast. A one-hour drama is shot every eight days. The scripts roll in late, sometimes two days before shooting. So it's a frenzy to get it cast. Actors with quick study skills get TV roles because they stay sharp and study their craft in an acting or audition class every week. Feature film auditions, we have more time. So the actor has more time. There is no casting judgment of an actor with a short prep time or a long prep time; there only is a prepared actor who takes the time allowed to perfect the audition."

So what's the best strategy to succeed given short turnaround? Craig Campobasso suggests using the Meisner doable actions he discussed earlier. Of course, I also urge you to constantly practice working with cold scenes on your own, too, so you aren't starting out with rusty skills.

Sue Winik also advises actors to constantly study and to work with a qualified coach for important auditions.

" Since sides are used for auditions in film and TV as well as some theater auditions, it is to an actor's advantage to work with a coach. A support system in this day and age is vital to an actor's success, but they must have the correct type of coach—one for theater and one for film/TV. Although the character preparation is much the same, the techniques are distinctly different and must be advised as such. This is why it is so important for an actor to be in class and perfecting his skills even if he has trained in the best school or conservatory. Skills must be sharp when you need them. Rehearsing with a school buddy or your roommate will not do. You need trained eyes. Also, an actor must be supremely prepared.

"Casting people consider an unprepared actor a waste of everyone's time. Lines or sides need to be memorized but not 'set'—so the actor can be open to adjustments from the casting director or director. Always carry sides into an audition. This is not a memorization exercise—also—if you don't carry the sides, they think this is the best you'll ever get without sides, and even if you have potential, they can pass over you. You may/may not refer to the sides as you need or like."

GETTING IN FOR AUDITIONS AND MARKETING

I have found that if you have strong marketing tools and present yourself professionally, you can get auditions even without agents. Craig Campobasso agrees.

"A good actor is a good actor whether they are represented or not. But how are you going to get seen if you have no representation? If this is the case, do casting director workshops to meet CDs who cast TV and film. They are always looking for fresh faces. I see actors unrepresented all the time. Some book the role. But it is important to be represented. Your face will get out more to all CDs in town."

Caroline Sinclair advises how actors can be seen without an agent.

"The best ways for actors to get auditions with me is usually through recommendations. If an agent that I respect calls up, I will always see that person. If the person does not have an agent, the best way is to invite me to a play or showcase. Also, I quite like being sent postcards with notices of what the person is up to. That is a fairly painless way. Also, actors are welcome to e-mail. In addition, I often call in actors that I meet at seminars. I feel that as long as the places are legitimate and most of these networking places are at least in New York City, it is a very good and safe place for actors with no representation to meet casting directors."

Sue Winik talks about how agents and actors can work together to maximize career opportunities.

"Many actors feel that since they have an agent, they can now sit back because the agent will do everything for them. *Wrong!!!* When you have an agent, this person is your partner in your business. Especially if you are not well-known, you want to make it as easy as possible for your agent to get you seen. These are things an actor needs and needs to do:

- Website
- One-on-one meetings
- Postcards

"Don't call, drop by, be generally annoying, or e-mail your agent or casting people continually."

Brian Gramo says that having a fan base is essential if you want to be cast in a webisode series. You need to get exposure in that world to impress producers.

"Generally, if you're a webisode, it's because you don't have the budget to be a miniseries or a special presentation on Showtime or

HBO or something on real TV, so you're working at a lower budget, so you're almost trying to cast a rock star, you're trying to cast a lead singer of the band. Yeah, a lot of people can sing well, but are they a rock star?

"You could be the best actor out there and you might get beat by someone that's not as good as you, but they have more Twitter followers than you, or they've been in more Web series than you. They're just more relevant. So having a presence and maintaining your own fan base, and, like I said, being a little bit of a rock star, that's one more thing you're bringing to the Web series 'cause it's not just showing up and being a good actor. In fact, being a good actor sometimes has nothing to do with it."

PROTOCOL FOR WEBISODE AUDITIONS AND PRODUCTIONS

Traditionally, actors seek auditions through casting directors or *Back Stage* magazine. These methods may not be used as much with webisodes because the budgets are smaller. Brian Gramo, therefore, suggests that actors should make connections with their social networking groups, such as Facebook, LinkedIn, and Twitter. He says to explore sites for meetups such as Tubefilter. Gramo suggests that you look into live sites like these that you can talk to people: theStream.tv, Ustream.tv, stickam.com, and livestream.com. He also points out that you can talk to people, comment, and reply via video on YouTube. In short, new sites will emerge so stay current and keep searching.

Gramo also urges actors to go to events that webisode producers and directors will attend. He says to check out the International Academy of Web Television and attend conventions like Comic-Con, E3 Expo, and South by Southwest (SXSW). Organized functions offer terrific networking opportunities for actors.

Brian Gramo elaborates: "If you really want to get into Web video, first of all pick a bunch of Web series that you like, that you aspire to be like, that you can draw inspiration from and see where they're going—they're going to conventions, trust me. Go to those conventions, see what they're doing, meet them, say 'hi,' don't be a stalker, and just see what other people are doing and mimic that because they're doing those things for a reason because it works."

Gramo says a performer must be realistic and come prepared for anything on a webisode shoot. He emphasizes, "Don't be a diva. Bring what you need. Don't expect them to have the meal that you need. Don't expect them to have all the stuff and don't ask for stuff."

Webisode productions demand disciplined actors who can perform on any location. Often productions have smaller crews and may be shot in real locations so actors must be very focused on the work at hand. Remember, time is precious so be ready to perform on cue.

Brian Gramo: "You have to be incredibly good at acting because you're going to find that you don't have the crew support that you will have in a higher-level production. Here's what I mean by crew support. In a higher-level production, you're going to have a lot more protection from the environment around you. So if you can't stay focused when there's a lot of sound distractions and when there's a lot of traffic distractions, or just people that aren't very familiar with being on set—you know, they might say the wrong thing or they might be too noisy. You're going to have a hard time as opposed to someone that can really block everything out, particularly if they have to get emotional, and let's say, cry. Because the lower budget situation you are in, the less amenities you're going to have as far as being a coddled protected actor."

Although collaboration is encouraged, it's also important for actors to respect the director's role on the set. Don't waste valuable production time with every little idea. Weigh what is helpful and just egoistical.

Brian Gramo: "The most annoying thing is when an actor tries to turn into the director. Like I said before, anyone that's working on a project should be open and willing and seeking collaboration and some feedback. But there comes a point where too much is bad and you can be nagging. I've definitely worked with actors where you'll do a take and they'll stop so many times to say, 'Hey, you know, wouldn't it make sense to do this, and wouldn't it make more sense to do that?' that it turns into a lack of trust for the other people that have set up the imaginary situation that you're in."

Breaking in to any new field is exciting and challenging, but you must be realistic about learning the ropes. Gramo shares tips that are useful for any area of the business you want to explore. He says you should try to check out other crew positions on a production to get to know people and understand how to work on a set. Be a production assistant, for example, if you are just starting out. Once you get a job, show up on time or early so that people know that you are reliable. You need experience, so in the beginning, do as much as you can to build a resume.

Brian Gramo: "When you're just starting out, you can't be so judgmental about the project where, you know, you're not willing to do it. And the first couple things you do might not be amazing and they might not be ideal situations, and just use it as a war story for later . . . and then once you have some things under your belt, then maybe you can start to be a little selective about your direction. But until you can get out there and make some contacts, . . . you can't be too picky, . . . try to get yourself some tape and with the way things are digital nowadays, you really got to make sure you got that tape. . . .

"Bring a hard drive and transfer it. Everyone's doing everything digitally nowadays. So if you can get some footage, even if you don't have the final edit, if you can get a little footage that day, particularly if you're not getting paid, definitely go for it."

As new technologies emerge, always study the field and find out who the key players are who can cast you. Learn about what skills will be needed for each unique shoot and create the best promotional tools you can to pitch your skills to potential buyers.

TRADITIONAL AND DIGITAL MEANS OF MARKETING

Getting your picture out professionally will also increase your chances of being seen. Craig Campobasso offers some tips on how to market: "Actors should have their reels and pics and resume on sites like Actors Access through breakdown services, LA Casting, Casting Networks, Now Casting, etc. It's easy and [available] to us at a click of a mouse."

Stewart F. Wilson-Turner is a vice president with Voicebank. net (www.voicebank.net) that links producers and agents digitally. Voicebank enables agents to send video auditions to clients much like individual actors post their auditions on Actors Access.

Wilson-Turner says, "Actors audition for clients with Voicebank through their agents. They can go to their agent's office and do as many auditions (audio, video, or print) as the agent has for them. The agent then uploads and distributes the auditions to the appropriate producers or casting directors."

As Stewart F. Wilson-Turner observes, this is becoming very popular because it streamlines the casting process.

"Producers like Voicebank because it connects them directly to the talent agencies who represent and know their clients and their capabilities the best. As the actor pool grows, producers will look to the strong relationships they have and trust with agents they've worked with before. Also, as budgets get tighter, the ability to hire a casting director for a 'small' [budget] job becomes less likely, opening up a talent agency's opportunity to audition directly since many do not charge for auditions."

Actors have many options to submit videotaped auditions via the Internet. Stewart F. Wilson-Turner explains how each service works.

"The difference between Actors Access and Voicebank is the postings on Actors Access are generated from casting directors who don't mind receiving self-submissions from actors. Postings on Voicebank go directly to agents, not actors. The agent auditions the actor, then uploads the video clip themselves."

So whether you work with your agent or do an audition on your own, it's good to be ready to help producers see your work fast and economically. Here are the formats Wilson-Turner suggests you should use for your auditions.

"The best video format to submit for an audition is QuickTime (.mov). All Macs can play it and any PC can easily download and install the player. It's also the most user-friendly format."

WHAT DO AGENTS WANT?

Author Dale Carnegie suggests in his book *How to Win Friends & Influence People* that you should think about what a potential boss wants. The same rule can be applied to actors seeking agents. You need to consider what you can do for an agent. Fortunately Sue Winik has some wonderful tips for you too.

"Agents are always looking for *trained* talented people. What constitutes talent in one person's eyes is not talent in another person's eyes. This is an amazingly subjective business.

"Agents are always looking for interesting people to supplement their talent pool. If I already have two twentysomething blond girls, I will not be interested in other twentysomething blond girls unless there is something so incredibly special or unique about the new girls. I may have only one Asian twentysomething young man and want to have at least three because that is what seems to be in the breakdowns this year. So any [Asian] twentysomething young man has a pretty good chance of getting called in by me.

"Occasionally I will take a chance on an inexperienced actor, but I am always careful to try not to send him into something that I feel would be over his head. Some actors are worth cultivating."

Individual agents have their own tastes and you have to find one that "clicks" for you. Personalities come into play because you'll have such a close relationship with an agent. Sue Winik describes her preferences when selecting actors.

"Personally, I favor trained actors who have [a] strong improv and sketch comedy background. I like people who have an offbeat sense of the world. I like people with warm personalities. (If I have to talk to you three or four times a day, I don't want to dread it.) I like actors who are serious about their business and will partner with me in trying to find projects for them. I like people who are well-spoken and have the right tools to succeed, i.e.: excellent pictures with resumes attached, the appropriate coaches, are in classes, have day jobs that allow flexibility so the actor can go on auditions . . . and own[s] a watch to always be on time!

"I like to hear monologues in my office so I can see that an actor knows how to prepare. I like to talk a lot to the actor to know them as people so I get a sense of who they are and where they fit in with the people I like to represent.

"I like people who are loyal and honest with me. (This sort of sounds like a marriage . . . and it is like that)."

Your agent is on your team and you should support them in every way you can. Sue Winik stresses how important it is for actors to take an active role in marketing and shaping their career.

"It is very important in this new electronic age of submissions, personal relations between the casting people and agents are coming into a different age. Anything you can do will be helpful in putting your face in front of the casting person.

"Networking with fellow working actors is good too. It keeps you in the loop of things happening. The operative word is *working*. I always tell my actors to not hang around friends that are *not* working. Working people have a better attitude and seem to have more insight as to where the new work is coming from."

I hope these interviews have shed some light on how you can be better prepared to win auditions if you want to work professionally. Even if you don't want to compete, so to speak, it's great to reach for higher goals all the time because you never know when an opportunity will arise. Too many actors get out of shape and aren't ready when an offer comes up, so take the time to reevaluate your own goals and your acting skills from time to time to make sure you won't miss a great chance to play the perfect part.

10

Working Toward
Your Career Goals

Charting a course for a career is essential. Goals should be simple and practical. If you want to be a movie star within a year and you've never acted, then you may be off base. On the other hand, if you have a realistic idea of your budget and set aside funds for acting costs, then you're on a good path.

You will have to invest in whatever is needed to give you a professional advantage. Classes, headshots, and speculative auditions require time and money. Therefore, be realistic about your schedule and the funds you can spare. You should seek appropriate parts. Every medium dictates different types, so you need to study suitable roles in each performance arena. Ask people for advice if you aren't sure where you fit in best.

Many actors lack the discipline to practice their craft and stay in shape. You should resist these tendencies. If you decide to try to perform in professional situations, then you need to develop home workouts or attend regular classes. You'll want your wardrobe neat and organized and your appearance well maintained. In addition, you'll want to be fit, flexible, and in good shape. Although the aforementioned may seem obvious, many actors can get lax. It is no easy feat to act on a regular basis, audition, study, and keep a good, steady survival job. Often, parts are yours to lose. The final goal, of course, will be to support yourself as an actor.

In order to be ready to book jobs, you should have a vision or an overall plan for your career. This can include long-range goals. Perhaps you want to book a commercial, a TV role, or join a theater group within a year. Whatever your desires, you need to consider why you want to act. Is it because you love it, or do you think you'll get rich? If you love something, you'll generally stick with it.

MAKING CONNECTIONS

Strong marketing and networking tools are important ways to advertise your talents to buyers. If you're just starting out, you'll want to use close friends for leads to industry connections. Reputable casting directors can often recommend acting academies too. Adult education programs and community colleges may be resources for classes as well. Unions also often offer free or low-cost workshops, especially in New York and Los Angeles. Regional theaters may be good places to meet actors—don't be afraid to volunteer as an usher to get to know people if you're not ready to audition for the group.

The Internet offers tools for actors to market their skills and submit headshots for parts. Actors Access (www.actorsaccess.com) and LA Casting (www.lacasting.com) are examples of such Websites. Both list auditions for roles online, and LA Casting has many commercial auditions listed. You can also check out Now Casting (www.nowcasting.com) and NY Castings (www.nycastings.com). SAG members can create marketing profiles with iActor as well (www.sag.org). Ask for recommendations of reputable sites, and remember, you'll usually pay a fee to submit your auditions. Finding a way to videotape your work on your own is increasingly helpful, as more submissions can be done online.

If you are just starting out, try to do student films to break into the business. Webisodes featuring short scripted episodes for the Internet also offer recurring and single-play roles as an alternative to the unscripted reality TV programs (which do have casting calls). You can also find leads for parts with Backstage.com and Entertainment-careers.net. Always use good judgment when submitting for these parts. Do your best to find reputable projects.

Make sure you have a strong marketing packet too. Your picture should be a good representation of you. Study a range of headshots and interview at least three photographers when you're getting your first pictures. Remember, you need to feel very comfortable with the person shooting you—so don't rush it. Again, ask friends, classmates, or teachers for strong recommendations for the best photographers.

WORKING WITH CASTING DIRECTORS

Casting directors open many doors for actors. They are gatekeepers between you and directors or clients. You need to, therefore, become familiar with casting directors in your area. Some casting directors will see you only for commercial auditions. Others will cast for film or TV projects. You may read parts directly for theater producers or directors.

It's important to understand how busy these people are. They often have little turnaround time to prepare for auditions. Producers and directors will seek qualified casting people to narrow down their search for a part. You are, therefore, lucky to go to auditions that may have a smaller pool of candidates.

Keep in mind that casting directors constantly look at reels, pictures, and auditions so you need to stand out as a professional. Don't ask questions that are already answered on a script. Take direction well and be polite. Be punctual. Know your part if time permits. Play your lines to the camera so that a director can see your acting.

Try your best to get to know casting directors who can get you auditions for roles you are likely to book. You need to market yourself to casting directors so they know who you are before they start their massive casting process, which could include 1,000 actors. It's crucial, therefore, to know all the key players in the casting offices and send them postcards to stay on their radar.

Back Stage magazine or online will have information about casting directors. Also, Castingabout.com is an online site that offers great comprehensive tools for actors to research and efficiently market to casting directors in New York and Los Angeles, because it is regularly updated with the latest developments in the industry. You can refine your search to create categories that suit your needs and even print out mailing labels. This site saves time and energy, because it provides the most current listings. You'll know when casting people move to different productions or are promoted to new positions. This helps you to talk about what casting directors are doing instead of always having to focus on yourself. Write postcards focusing on what *they* are doing and go to a casting audition knowing who is at the front desk. Show a genuine interest in what the casting assistant is up to and they may remember you for years to come. In short, don't wait to hear about the perfect role; get to know casting directors so they think of you first.

If you don't live in Los Angeles or New York, go online and search for professionals in your region if you can't find them in the trades. Become familiar with what kind of projects they cast. Then you should try to attend any seminars or classes they offer to meet them and showcase your work. Once you establish contact, you can stay in touch with postcards highlighting your recent work. You don't want to hound people—just give them reminders that you are working or congratulate them on their latest accomplishment.

As stated before, in some instances casting directors may bring you in for an audition even if you don't have an agent. Use every means, therefore, to give them your best performance. If you impress someone, they may even lead you to an agent. In a nutshell, make friends with casting directors because they can be helpful to you throughout your career.

FINDING AN AGENT

As you seek an agent, you should be ready for anything. Have a few monologues prepared just in case you're asked to perform them and make sure your cold scene reading skills are up to snuff. Generally, agents only take ten percent of any earnings you book through their auditions, but a manager gets fifteen percent of all of your performance earnings. Percentage rates can always vary so check current agent and manager fees if you are not aware of industry standards. You should never pay an agent for anything else—it is unethical. Also keep in mind that the agent works for you. They do ten percent of the work and you do ninety percent of the work. An agent will get auditions for you and only take ten percent of what you earn for those auditions when you book a job. Managers help you with your overall career and may suggest classes or even help you secure an agent. They will work with you and an agent on a game plan for your career. Even if you have an agent or manager, you still need to constantly study, market your talents to buyers, and show up to your auditions on time and behave professionally.

How do you obtain an agent? There is no simple answer, but there is a surefire way to impress someone. Prove that you are a professional actor capable of making money. Demonstrate strong performance skills; show that you are you are willing to work hard, and that you are personable. Getting an agent is like getting a job. Referrals can open doors, but there is no guarantee that you'll be picked up by the agency. The best way to succeed is to know the playing field and to be ready to perform on a moment's notice.

Don't be intimidated by agents or conversely, feel entitled to representation. Be yourself and remember you're actually auditioning the agent to represent *you*. So you want to like him and his business style. Study the talent rosters of agents before you go to an interview. Find the best agent for your current needs. Smaller boutique agencies don't have as many auditions but you may get more individual attention. On the other hand, large agencies have clout even if you are not on the top rung of their roster. Decide what is best for your needs and go after it.

Being organized is very important. You may get a call for an audition a few hours or days before your appointment. Don't waste time. Get to work on your part as soon as you can. Select your wardrobe and have it ready the day before if possible. Allow plenty of time to drive and park. Try to avoid being late—especially in Los Angeles, don't be the clichéd actor. If you are a professional actor, keep good financial records of all your expenses and earnings to maximize your bottom line.

Too many performers forget it's the entertainment *business*. If you want to succeed, then you'll have to be patient and persistent. You may have to audition a lot before you book a job. You may have to do unpaid theater work or student films to keep your skills honed if the industry is slow. Being on time, polite, sober, and prepared are the best ways to impress industry professionals. Even if you're not right for one role, casting directors may think of you for another one, so behave like a pro.

Build a support system of people who believe in your talents. Create a workout group to cut costs if you're an experienced actor. Voice actors do it all the time, but if you don't need to record the performances, you can save studio costs. All you need is a space and a group of actors willing to comment on each other's performances. You can even use online applications like iChat and Skype to work via camera remotely.

KEEP REFINING YOUR TALENTS AND BUSINESS PLAN

Create your own opportunities too: perform a one-person show, produce and act in a play, or create short films and webisodes. As you perform more, you'll meet people who can help you make industry connections.

No matter what you plan to do, you'll always want to forge ahead and explore new and challenging roles to keep your instrument strong. Remember, performing can be very fulfilling in and of itself. Even if you just love acting, you'll feed your creative spirit while doing other things. In the end, if you stay creative and strong, you'll be ready for the next role, and who knows where it might take you?

If you want to act, then perform. It's that simple. No agent or manager will give you drive and ambition if you don't care about the craft. You have to love doing it so much that you'll find ways to make it happen. Does that sound harsh? Then maybe you should rethink your goals.

I attended an agent seminar hosted by the American Federation of Television and Radio Artists (AFTRA). The agents expressed their desires to the group. Agents need actors who are active and ready to work. While they are out there judging your talent in student films, theater, webisodes, and showcases, showing drive and passion and professionalism makes their job easier.

Taking classes proves that you're serious and you are working at your skill set too. You can't suddenly learn how to do a part the day before an audition. You must be actively creating parts so that you are ready. This means that you can quickly learn lines because you're always working on roles and that you have headshots and wardrobe on hand to market your talents.

You may find it is difficult to juggle everything. A career can be sabotaged if you don't have a reliable survival job or are unrealistic about what you can and can't do. After my son was born, I did an improv show because I didn't have the time to do theater. There are always avenues to explore: play readings, performing in schools, or volunteering your skills for a community reading. You can always read and rehearse parts on your own and perhaps record them if you have equipment.

Read biographies of famous actors to study the journey they traveled. Draw inspiration and lessons from their stories of triumph and defeat. Even stars have had a lull in their careers. Sometimes you may need to take a break too. Distance can bring things into focus. However, laziness can create a dead-end career.

Pretend you're an agent or manager and really examine your acting package. How good are your marketing tools? Do they reflect your most suitable character type? Does your reel bring out the best of your talents? How are you going to distribute your marketing packet?

Networking is one of the most powerful ways an actor can find out about what's happening in the industry and get new leads. Industry seminars or classes at your union are great ways to meet and greet people. Acting teachers can also point you in new directions. You can't do it alone; my career came about with the help of countless people.

Don't get stuck in a rut. Casting professionals and agents constantly appreciate it when actors keep working at their craft. At the very least, you'll expand your skills and contacts. Also, don't forget to study marketing and sales campaigns. Really be clinical and figure out what strategies work effectively to deliver a message. Advertising is subtle and psychological. Using the *six degrees of separation* idea, start by telling your friends about your acting accomplishments. First, you might tell a friend that you are doing a showcase. Then you'll mention that you are in a student film. Finally, you'll chat about another accomplishment and suddenly your friend may think of someone who is looking for an actor. You have to put your talents out there and find ways to stand out in the field. Also, you never know when someone is looking for a performer, so reminding them from time to time can increase your chances of making a connection.

On the other hand, take your time to be professional. Do your research and know the name of the agent you are sending your letter to rather than addressing it: To Whom It May Concern. Make sure that you have proofread everything and that it looks professional. Don't ever misrepresent your skills. Also, only send as many inquiries as you can follow up on; otherwise, don't waste your time. It is better to do good research, seek companies that would be a good match for you, and write a terrific letter than to send one hundred headshots and lose track of everything.

Getting an agent is like getting a job, so read books on sales and marketing to polish your presentation. Picture what it would be like to have one hundred headshots on your desk. Then imagine how the first line of a well-conceived letter can catch an agent's eye and be a relief. Agents want to be able to bring in good, new talent, but they have very little time because they have to get work for their current clients, so make your presentation worth their efforts. Make their day—don't waste their precious time.

An acting career is not something that may happen overnight, so be patient. Also remember why you got into this in the first place—

that it's a lot of fun to pretend and play different roles. Allow yourself permission to enjoy the learning process too. It's easy to sabotage your efforts because you feel that you haven't landed the dream part. Stop and rethink your current goals. Are you being unrealistic? Do you need to be further along to play a certain role, or is it not right for you? If you are appropriate for a part, then figure out why your competition is getting the work. There are also times when you are not right for roles, and you have to be patient and wait for the perfect audition to surface.

Stay positive and see yourself working and performing parts that are well within your grasp. Accept your strengths and minimize your weaknesses. Also understand that many actors don't work full time, and that you have to create ways to support your artistic lifestyle.

Above all, enjoy the rehearsal process you do on your own and unearth new characters and untapped skills. Stay abreast of new technologies so you'll be on the forefront of emerging acting opportunities. Don't wait for job opportunities to disappear, always learn about the latest trends so you can keep growing. Be ready to act so that when the call for that perfect part comes, all of your hard work will pay off both literally and figuratively.

11

Monologues and Improvisation Exercises

In this section you will have a variety of monologue scripts to experiment with and explore. There are no character descriptions or scene setups, so you need to be creative. You will have to fill in the blanks and make as many specific choices as you can based on the information you are given. The scripts are designed with specific challenges, and study notes are provided to help you tackle each one.

These are exercises to help you work with isolated scenes that provide few clues, so you must discover as much as you can from the text that is provided. In addition, these scripts offer a range of situations and characters so that you can stretch and make new discoveries about the types you are best suited to play. Tap into your imagination and have fun with these scenarios.

THE CODE

It's right here. I know I wrote it down (fumbling in wallet or purse). I don't know where it is. Oh, it's on the tip of my tongue. There are so many of these things. Was it Barneys—that was where we met—well, I know they tore it down—but we went there all the time.

No, oh, let me think. I don't know why it's not here. I save everything. You know, like wedding vows and promises you make when you're young. Because they just don't last. You think they will, but something happens.

Maybe it's Pierre's; that was where we used to have our anniversary dinners. Try that. We would say how much we loved each other and there was wine and romance. That's it—romance. Try that, because that's what's missing. I mean, how many hours can you work at a damn office? How long can you stay away from your spouse before they notice?

That's not it? Try deception. That's gotta work because it's all that's left. I mean there's polite conversation, distant stares at dinner, and an occasional peck on the cheek by the door in the morning.

No? Try divorce, that's gotta be the key. There are no other words or affairs or lies or lonely nights. Nothing else is going to work. I tried everything. I did. It's not my fault. It didn't open? Well, it works for me.

▶ Challenges: This is just about forgetting a code.
▶ Strategies: Your lack of control is a trigger that ignites your resentment and anger.

THAT'S IT?

That's it? I came all the way over here to say one lousy line and it's "Thank you for coming. Next?" No I don't think so—not this time, not today. Uh-uh!

No, no, let me say what I have to say. Do you even know how much time I spent on this? The research? The rehearsal? What about the hours of prep time? Huh? Not to mention the years of classes with divas—everything from diction to moving my little pinky just so? Oh, oh, and the theater work. We can't forget that, can we? The dinner theater where someone's pork chops take center stage over my big monologue. Not just any monologue, but the one I've been working on forever for agents to notice me—the one where I go from giddy to despair in the short span of a minute.

Hey, stop looking at me like I'm crazy! I know I'm crazy. I wait tables, answer phones, temp at just about anything for this chance to strut my considerable stuff!

You know, I did a weekend workshop at the Yale Drama School one summer. I've done improv. I can roll with the punches. I can make space come alive from nothing—not a single piece of furniture! I can create a full apartment down to a tiny teacup with my hands and my fine-tuned imagination. Just don't make me put on a clown costume, because I'm severely clown-phobic.

You want to watch me? There—(gives questionable gesture)! That's how it goes. Oh, come on, can't you read sign language? I'd be happy to sing a few bars of a ballad. I certainly spent enough money on singing lessons.

(Clears throat.) What's that? You think I'm perfect? You mean I'm finally getting to say a line? (Smiles.) I knew I nailed it. Yeah!

- ▶ Challenges: It's easy to portray this as a clichéd actor and to play at the character.
- ▶ Strategies: Make very specific choices for your beats. Try to use your own real yearnings and desires to be an actor to make this sincere and urgent.

WINTER

I wish the spring was at my back and I was going into the summer. There would be light and long days and I could face it. But the winter is so bitter cold and the harsh wind haunts me.

Why didn't I prepare for this situation? Did I think I could escape it? Oh, I wish it were the end of summer, when you're ready for the cold rush on your face. The wind is a tonic, and not a thief stealing away every breath.

In winter, the bare branches scrape at the window at night like chalk on a blackboard and it keeps you from feeling warm under the covers or certain about the daylight coming. There is too much darkness and my soul feels the chill of this black night.

I can't sleep anyway, until I find out where I'm going next. Fear is a funny thing—it, not cancer, can kill you. They told me I'd have to move out before the end of the month. At least if it were the fall, I'd have the crisp smell of cider in my nose and the memory of brilliant leaves falling on carefree school days—but no, I face it alone in this winter.

This is where I was going to stay. It's where I wanted to be, but I can't fight the forces of nature and greed. I never was much of a fighter. I was happy to let things go, and I guess that is why I'm losing everything now. I pray at night and I know someone hears me. You have to take your strength where you can get it—even if the sun seems to have vanished from the sky—but I don't know where I'm going tomorrow or the next day or after that. And I'm afraid.

▶ Challenges: This is heavy formal writing. It's not conversational.
▶ Strategies: Figure out why this situation has happened. Understand the specifics about what went wrong and what fate awaits the character. Do a detailed backstory.

LITTLE

Shhhh, Dad will hear us. He said we had to be quiet. He said he meant it this time. Oh, don't cry! Then he'll really get mad.

He yelled at Mom earlier today, so you don't want him to come in here. Move here, under the table where it's safe. There are no mean people here. This is the place where we can escape.

See, here's a flashlight for the night. This is where I come whenever I am afraid and want to feel safe. Come on, don't cry! I'll take it this time. I'll tell Dad I broke it. Gee, I don't know why he'd be so mad anyway. It was a cheap little toy. Oh, come on, Billy, it's okay. Quiet down.

Let me see your arm. It looks okay. Here, let me take my magic wand to make your boo—boo disappear. (Flourishes flashlight as if it's a wand). There. There you go. Better? I thought so.

See, you just got to create a place where you're not so afraid. I used to be like you, but then I found this place. It's small like us. No one has to know our secret 'cause they might spoil it. So don't tell anyone.

He's got to go back to work tonight. I heard him talk to Mom. I guess it's her night. We'll see when he goes.

Oh don't worry—she's big. It's okay. She can take care of herself. But someday I'm going to be big and then I'll help her. Yes, I won't be little. I'll be as big as Dad then.

◗ Challenges: Here you must believe you are a child first. You are playing a child just like you might in a flashback scene in a play.
◗ Strategies: Understand the strong motivation to help your sibling. Recall what it is like to be innocent and dependent on adults.
◗ If this upsets you in any way, skip it.

NOT HOT

Hey, Bob, what's up? I heard you had a date with that hot chick down the hall. How'd that go? Not that I'm hard up. Gotta beat 'em off with a stick most days.

Oh, when you got it, you don't need to flaunt it. I know I'm modest, but look at the body—tight and firm. I can do chin-ups blindfolded no problem. The guys at the gym can't believe it, but the little ladies just look in awe and wonder when it will be their turn. They just line up. I know I'm a tease, but I can't please 'em all. I got to save myself for the super babes.

Oh, you know, the models, actresses, and bodybuilders. Why does everybody give me that look? I am a man who is very secure in my masculinity–I'm not afraid of a little steroid-induced strong-armed lady. It's a turn-on.

Those chicks make an Olympic sport out of foreplay. And stamina?! They're like that ever-always-ready bunny on batteries charged from some nuclear waste site. Oh, it's so hot to think about it. I might need a cold shower now.

Hey, throw me what ya' got on tap! I've worked up a thirst here. Hold on. Can you believe that one over there—legs that won't stop and she wants me. I know she does. I can see it in her pliable body language. I'm sensitive like that. She's beggin' for it.

(Gets up from the bar.)

Well, I'm not cruel. I can make a lady purr when she wants to be wound up like a sex toy. Watch how the doctor makes a love call. Wait—what's this—another lady movin' in? Now, this is the challenge I've been living for. Don't wait up.

- ◗ Challenges: This character seems like a total jerk and unreal. The temptation is to be broad.
- ◗ Strategies: Dig deeper. Find the flaws and pain that drives a person to behave this way. Do *as ifs* using times when you were a jerk. Also think of how insecurities can make you behave badly.

150 BUCKS

Wait, you're telling me it's going to cost one hundred and fifty bucks to fix this? I just bought it a year ago and now it's broken! I paid seven hundred dollars for it—but of course that doesn't matter now, because the warranty has expired. Well, I'm not going to do that. I'll find someone else who won't try to take advantage of me. I walk in here and you think you can just pull something over on me? No way!

I'm treated that way all the time. People think just because I look like this, they don't have to play by the rules, because somehow all bets are off. Well, for your information they aren't and you should be ashamed of yourself. Who are you going to cheat next week huh—an old lady?

You'd make your own mother pay retail. You have no shame— but this time you don't get the sale! I'll find someone who will not see me as prey. I'm sick of people trying to kick me because they think they can. So you can kiss my business goodbye!

▶ Challenges: You have very general ideas to work with in this monologue.
▶ Strategies: Make a choice about why people take advantage of you. Also, create a high-stakes reason this money is so important to you. Why is the object being repaired so important?

TIGHT

What do you think? Oh, I know it's a little snug here and I could take a bigger size, but I don't feel like it today. The color's right, and I don't want to wear something with a label that says Large. You know?

No, of course you don't. Look at you—so skinny! Oh, let me guess, you eat like a horse and don't work out. You never get on the scales and you always look like that. You were just born with it, so you're lucky—and that makes me unlucky because I wasn't born with a body that burns calories like crazy or looks good in the latest fashion. No, I have to settle for whatever comes in my size—and God forbid a designer would ever spend the time to create something for someone like me. No, I gotta take what I can get and hope that someone will be blind or will need something so bad that they won't be ashamed to be with me.

Who am I kidding? No one's gonna want to be with me anymore if I wear this or if I wear the super large size. I can't hide it with a fabric that pinches my skin—but at least I can pretend for a minute that I'm like everyone else I see, and I can believe that the way I look doesn't matter.

▶ Challenges: If you are overweight, this can hit a nerve. If you are underweight, this is a stretch.

▶ Strategies: If you are overweight, let your resentments build and be subtle. If you are thin, use the resentment others have toward you to fuel your feelings.

LAST CHANCE

Oh, my god, I can't believe I tripped like that! I don't know what's wrong with me. Thanks for helping me pick up these papers. I can't be late today. No, Rob needs the report and this is my last chance of making up for a less-than-stellar year.

I heard they've fired six people from the seventh floor. I have no idea why I'm telling you this. I don't know what's wrong with me. Well, yep, I actually do. This is my fifth job in five years and I guess I just get a little nervous when I hear the words "laid off" or "fired" or "we don't need you anymore."

It's like déjà vu all over again. "Please sit down, there's no easy way to say this, so I'll just say it." Then I think, *why me*? Why not your brother-in-law, or your secretary that you're well, ya know, or the Sr. V.P. who gets drunk at lunch and leaves early most days? What did I do wrong this time? Oh, yeah, I didn't play the game.

So what! I'm not great at office politics. I admit it, but I do good work. Oh hell, who cares, that has nothing to do with it. It's just a popularity contest—but being unpopular means I don't get to eat.

▶ Challenges: You start off vulnerable.
▶ Strategies: Build a detailed life story as a career loser but also raise the stakes. Make this time different from other firings in some crucial way.

FOUR O'CLOCK

Yes, can you at least check it? Well, no, I can't get on the Internet, because everyone is on the Internet now so my DSL goes down every day around four o'clock. I know I paid the bill. Why can't you stop sending me notices? Like I have better things to do than to call you to fix your mistake!

Look, I know you're online, but I can't get on to check it, so will you please just do it for me? It's your mistake, not mine! I got too many things to do and this is just one more thing. It's Smith—S-m-i-t-h. The account number is 54921009. What do you mean, you can't find it? That's your only job! I got a boss breathing down my neck to finish a report that was due yesterday and a sick husband/wife at home, and now I gotta pick up my kid in a few minutes. Will you please just reconnect the phone so when I run late they won't leave my kid alone outside in the rain?!

What do you mean, I have to send you my bank statement?! Screw it! I'll pay it now and fix it later just like everything else. What do you mean there is a fee?! YOU made the mistake!!!

Oh, forget it, I gotta pick up my kid. Do you take Visa?

▶ Challenges: You need to be befuddled and calm and then lose it.
▶ Strategies: Decide what has created your fog of denial and what triggers your jolt into reality.

PASSWORD

(Standing over a computer.)

Oh, I don't know what it is. Chester? That was the first street we lived on before we moved into our new house. I can't remember the name of it. Hell, I can't remember anything anymore. There are too many passwords. It's all a jumble. Did I pay my mortgage? What did I have for dinner last night? It's all a mess of mashed-up memories.

I don't live. I get up, eat, work, and go back to sleep. It's a grind, but I gotta do it. You know, a family has to survive in this overpriced world.

You're kidding! That didn't work? Well, can you open the site? I didn't know that. I can't cover the check. No, I can't use the savings. We're strapped. I'm gonna lose my house—that's what's gonna happen. I shoulda put my foot down. I shoulda said, "No, let's keep renting," but I gave in to the American dream—more like a nightmare.

What are you saying? I gotta make the payment today? They're laying off a whole division at the office. What's going to happen then? No, we can't borrow anymore. I told you we're broke.

Who am I kidding? We've had this behemoth on the market for a year. We HAVE brought down the price! The bank keeps calling about a foreclosure.

Forget the damn password! I'll see if I can get it from my brother. No password is going to solve this.

▶ Challenges: You need a sense of urgency that builds.
▶ Strategies: Use a situation in your own life to relate to this predicament. See the tech problem of hitting a wall as a metaphor for your character's desperate situation.

MEMORIES

What are you saying? You're going to put me in a home because you think that it's right for you? Well, I'm not going anywhere. I can see straight, think right, and stand on my own. Who put you up to this—that horrid (husband/wife) of yours? You don't have a mind of your own. You're a slave to that monster.

Well, I'm not giving you the power of attorney. You know, I still have a lawyer. But I suppose you'd love to have my house and things right? Don't look at me like that. I know who put you up to this—that conniving. . . . I should have stopped your marriage, but what good would that have done?

Who are you? I don't know you. Who did I raise? I didn't raise you. Maybe I just gave you too much; you're so damn lucky and lazy. That's right, lazy. You never worked for anything! And now you think you can just take my house and things to please your greedy spouse.

I guess I had this coming. I should have said no more often. I should have made you work harder. I should have stopped the marriage. But I didn't, and here I am looking at a kid I never raised and don't know.

Maybe you're right, maybe my memory is fading because I don't know who you are or why I let you in my house.

- ◗ Challenges: If you are older, this can be frightening to ponder. If you're younger, it's a big stretch.
- ◗ Strategies: If you are older, use your community of friends and family to identify with the character. If you are younger, explore the life of your older relatives and try to understand what it is like to have your life derailed or to be told where to live.

THE KEYS

Mom, come on. It's not that bad, really. You can't drive anymore. You almost killed someone! Do you want to spend the rest of your life in jail? Because that is what will happen, they won't let you off because you're old.

I love you (the mom glares), you know I do, but things have to change. This house is too big and you're too far away from anyone. It's not safe. You can't make me feel bad about this, because I can't have you killing someone or yourself on the road.

Don't look at me like that. I'm not doing anything bad to you. It's just where you are in life. You know, your memory isn't what it used to be, that cop said you had been driving for ten minutes before he could stop you.

It's time to make a change. You can move closer to us and live in a nice apartment with other people just like you. It's NOT an old folks' home. It's assisted living. They do everything for you. You won't need to drive. You said you hardly know anybody here anymore anyway.

Now, where did you put your keys? I know you've hidden them. Well, you can't stay here until I find them. You can't be here alone anymore. It's just not safe. Don't give me that look; it's not going to work. I fell for it too many times before. We've run out of options, so hand them over.

> ◗ Challenges: You have to understand the difficulty of the role reversal of a child and parent.
> ◗ Strategies: Build a strong sequence of events that makes this a point of no return. There are no other options.

CAUGHT IN THE ACT

(On the phone.)

Hey, babe, what time are you coming home? It's getting late and I'm hungry. You said you were working late, but this is ridiculous. Give me a call (hangs up).

Yeah, late with your little office mate—don't think I don't know what is going on there. It doesn't take a detective to uncover your lies. Where did I go wrong? I've been blindsided! I didn't see it coming. Then bam, like that—it's over! What does (he/she) have that I don't? Sex, that's what!

(Into the phone.)

Could you at least have the courtesy to call me back (slams phone). Forget it. I'm going down there. It's the only way to prove I'm right. I'll catch you on the desk or floor or wherever. I'll walk in on the "work" you're doing.

Don't think I don't hear you laughing on the phone when I call. The kind of laugh you make when you share something intimate with someone.

(On the phone.)

Hey. Oh, it's you. Where are you? Till midnight?! What's that I hear in the background? It sounds like you're in a nightclub. Client? What client do you have that would go to a place like that?

I'll meet you there. Hang on let me get the address. What do you mean you can't talk? Wait!

That's it! There aren't that many places you could be. I'll find you, and when I do, I'll catch you in the act. Next time you lie to me, it will be to my face!

▸ Challenges: Make the disconnection the character feels very real.
▸ Strategies: Use the distance of the phone to add to the disadvantage. Also consider all the good times the couple had together and why it's so important not to lose this relationship.

THE AGENT

Go ahead, kid, I don't have all day. Spit it out. Come on. I don't have time for this. Are you going to speak? Can you speak? What did ya come to this town for anyway—to be famous? Or was it to get rich? Think of something—now's your moment to deliver.

Where did ya come from—a small town? And now you're here to prove yourself? Or did you come from a broken home with no love? Is that it?

Well, this place won't give ya any of that. You're up against a labyrinth of liars and backstabbers waiting in the wings for you to trip up. There's always someone ready to seize your part like a leopard lying low ready to leap. It's every cliché you've ever heard. Yeah, it's a jungle, a rat race, a snake pit . . . so, why are you here?

Can't you figure it out? I don't have time for this. I got bills to pay and you're not ringing the dinner bell for me. Maybe you're Olivier or Bernhardt in your bedroom, but you gotta be able to fill a bigger space.

Don't you know your lines? Did you forget the part about wanting this so bad you'd do anything? You'd step on anybody and deceive yourself into believing nothing matters except being somebody in this town.

Well, let me tell you something. I am somebody. My time isn't cheap, and if you're not cut out for this, then go back to wherever you came from. Have no regrets! Because it isn't all it's cracked up to be unless you can look yourself in the mirror in the morning and stomach what you see. Go on, live your life. There's more out there than this town offers. Look, cheer up! Be glad you're facing it now. Better than when you're fifty and it's too late to leave. Ya know what I mean, kid?

> ◗ Challenges: This can be very clichéd.
> ◗ Strategies: Play against the stereotype. See an agent as a loving person in spite of the hard knocks. Also figure out what makes you so jaded by the business.

ROOMMATE HELL

Hey, I'm Betsy. Betsy Blound. My friends call me Bits. You can take the top bunk. I've got dibs on the bottom one. So this is it. I finally meet my first college roommate?! I'm so excited. I was .09 away from being valedictorian and I sang in every production our school ever did. That's how I got here.

I can't wait to get started and meet the professors. I always wanted to go here and now I've made it. Oh, I know it's competitive—but so am I. Do you want to play a game of Scrabble? I was in the high school championship. I love winning. It just feels so right.

Oh, you're reading that? I guess everybody needs to dumb it down before starting at this place. You look a little nervous—don't be, I can help you. I tutored kids after school—you know, underprivileged kids for my community service.

I'm really patient and a good listener as you can tell. Oh, if you're ever having a problem, I can help. I worked at a crisis phone center one summer as a volunteer. One kid killed himself, but he was a manic-depressive anyway. So you can always turn to me. I've had professional experience.

Oh, I've taken those drawers. I'm already unpacked. All my pencils are sharp. I'll be ready when I start my first class at eight AM tomorrow. You seem like a really easygoing person. I just know we're going to hit it off. Hey, where are you going? Wait up! I haven't told you about my family.

Don't leave me alone!

(The roommate leaves.)

Why does this always happen to me?

- ▶ Challenges: You can be tempted to play this character too broad.
- ▶ Strategies: Use the jitters of starting a new life and constant rejection by others to make a connection to something real. Feel free to adapt this to a male character.

FLIPPING THROUGH THE TV CHANNELS

The following monologues are inspired by television content, and therefore are shorter than the previous scripts. These scenarios cover a range of characters and genres to give you a lot of room to play. It is important to understand the styles, so study these shows. Don't ever play at characters—embrace their needs and wants. These diverse roles can help you stretch your skills and also find the parts that are within your comfort zone.

I don't give you a lot of scene or character descriptions because you should be able to glean the details from the scripts. The challenge here is for you to be creative and to think on your own. It's up to you to study media examples, and it's something you should be doing all the time anyway.

COMPETITION SHOWS

Everyone likes to be the very best at something, and the competition show satisfies this drive. Often, amateurs must demonstrate what they can do before a group of expert judges or, in some cases, the audience will cast a vote as well.

Emotions run high for both the hosts and the contestants. Think about how a professional would feel about an amateur attempting to break into the limelight to become a star in one fell swoop. Are they jealous? Did these judges ever have this chance at fame? Also, consider the exacting nature of the experts who love their craft. Nothing short of perfection will do. They only want the finest people in their high-profile fields.

Finally, remember how you behave in everyday life when someone points a camera at you. Often you will "mug" for the camera and act out. This frequently happens in both reality TV and competition shows. The contestants act out for the camera because they are not professional performers. Consider this discomfort, and be true to your character. Find sincere core emotions and build a strong backstory to justify your scenarios.

Host from Hell—Poor Taste

I didn't like the consistency. It was bitter too. The bleu cheese is too much for the delicate nature of this dish. I think if you want to remain on this show, to even continue as a chef, you're going to have to do better. There are so many more spices you could have added.

What about flavor? It was flat, and since your dish last week was a disaster, I'm afraid you'll have to go. Take your spatula and leave.

Fashion Flair

Oh, let me say the color and lines are extraordinary. I especially like the way it cinches at the waist and flares at the knees. You've also used wonderfully rich velvet that is different and fun. I think this is the perfect party dress for anyone at the holidays. I must say, you have surprised me! I didn't think *you* could pull it off. If you keep up this kind of catchy couture, you might make it to the finals. Congratulations!

Stumble with the Rumba

You call that a rumba? Where is the lust and the rhythm everyone expects? Your hips were too stiff, and you even missed a few beats. Then, when you added that lean back, you were *so* ungraceful. I can't imagine why you'd do a move like that unless you could pull it off. There isn't any connection between you two, either, and we talked about that last week, didn't we? I guess we'll see what the audience says. All I can add is that I gave you a 3. You have to do better to impress me.

Talent Galore

Oh, my god. That part with the dog was brilliant! Who knew a dog could play the accordion? Then, you chimed along on those water glasses while tap-dancing, which was a total surprise. Oh, but the snake flying through the air at the end and landing in the last water glass really took it to a new level. There is no doubt you have an act here that audiences will want to see again and again. I think I'm not alone when I say I'm proud and pleased to take you on to the finals, so you are coming back next week!

CRIME TIME

You can find any number of intriguing procedurals on TV that follow the path of a criminal. Passions are high and detectives are relentless in their pursuit of justice. We are fascinated with these shows because we love to try to solve the case, and we're drawn to the darker side of life because most of us don't experience it in our everyday lives.

Hatred, greed, insanity, abuse, and loss of love drive killers to their prey. These are intense justified emotions; so don't cheapen them with clichéd renditions of the scene. Don't put yourself above the law. Use your imagination to figure out situations that would trigger your anger to seek revenge or plot a murder. Understand a deranged character's odd mental quirks and see their world as they do.

In times of war and danger, we'd do many things we never would imagine we are capable of, and that's how you must approach the crime drama. Find real reasons your character either commits or fights crime. Cops often have experienced violence in their lives, so explore that angle too.

Revenge

He tore my dress and then grabbed me by the arm, and I couldn't get away. I begged him to stop but he threw me down and crushed my foot. The knife was right there and I grabbed it and stabbed him over and over again, but he wouldn't stop laughing. He kept saying his brother would find me and finish the job. That's why I got the gun. It wasn't supposed to go off when Bobby walked into the room, I thought that monster's brother had come back to finish the job. It was a mistake! You couldn't protect me. I had to do something!

First Prize

You always wanted the love and never got it from anyone. No matter what you did, your mother praised your brother. Your father never came to your games because you warmed the bench. That brother of yours stole the spotlight, and you hated him for that. Every trophy reminded you of every game. That was it, wasn't it? You killed him with the trophy because that's what you hated the most. It was the one thing that proved he was better than you. So you grabbed it while he was sleeping, hit him over the head, and then ransacked the apartment so that it would look like a robbery. There was no break-in, isn't that right? You killed him with that trophy, and then threw it off the bridge.

GAME SHOW

Name three things you eat for breakfast. Go! A game gets your adrenaline going because it's just plain fun to win something. We compete to prove we can beat the clock, opponent, or obstacle. There's a thrill or rush and a playful approach to the whole experience.

Contestants are "real people" from all walks of life. Please do remember, however, that these contestants, just like actors, are selected from many eager hopeful people. Understand why your character was selected. My husband and I appeared on the *Dr. Phil* show after being interviewed on the street because we were opposites. We were fun and entertaining because we made jokes about our differences. It was a totally random thing, but we were selected because our funny stories about life rang true for everyone.

Be a detective and figure out why the producer picked your character. Also, build a backstory for your role. Define your character's dreams, home life, and experiences watching the show. Figure out how your contestant plotted to get on the show. Finally, grasp the intense excitement of finally making it to your destination.

Theresa

I'm Theresa from Tulsa, and it took me five tries to get on the show, but I'm here to win it all. I've always wanted to win a horse race, and today I will make my dream come true to own a Triple Crown winner when I hit the jackpot. There is no one here who can stop me, because when I put my mind to it, I come through in the clutch. So, look out. I will make it through that maze faster than either of you because this is my moment to take it to the grand prize level. I've always wanted to have a horse compete at the Kentucky Derby, but I'm not stopping there. Look out, Secretariat, because I'm going all the way!

Ted

Um, I'm Ted Barker from a tiny town in Alaska called Weehop. The name kinda says it all, anyway. I'm hoping to take my taxidermy public and open a full-scale museum with all of my creatures. People don't realize what an art it is to bring every detail, from a tiny squirrel's foot to a big bobcat's tail, to life, and I want to share it with my neighbors, and hopefully the world. It's the kind of thing I think everyone will want to see. I'm ready to flip the switch to find out who I'm going to arm wrestle first to get to the finals. Bring it on!

Desperate

Well, Dave, my house is going to be taken away if I don't win here today, so I'm not walking out empty-handed. My wife is pregnant, and I've got two other kids, so I will not lose. I'm ready to run the gauntlet, and face the fire trail, paddle across the white water simulator, jump off twenty feet below, and grab that hundred-pound gold bar in two minutes flat. There's nothing stopping me from finishing first today. Whenever you're ready, just ring the bell and I'm off. My family is in the audience, and they know they can count on me, like they always have, until my job was outsourced and the factory closed. So let me show you how it's done!

Lone Housewife

This may sound funny, but I'm actually a housewife. I know, what's that? Well, my husband is a pilot, so he's never home for the family. I'm here because my sister's in town, watching the kids, and I've always wanted to solve the giant jigsaw. I mean, I always pick up the pieces at home, so why not, right? A little excitement never hurt anyone, or did it? (Giggles) Oh, I'm like that—always ready to have a good time, even though I'm alone most nights. Can't seem to get away much, but managed to make it here today, on TV no less. Look at me, kids. See what you can do with a little help from your family? You're never alone if you lean on your loved ones. So I'm not going home without that first prize. Let me pick out those pieces!

MEDICAL DRAMA

Life and death are the ultimate demarcations we face as humans. Usually we go about our business until someone or something threatens our very being. Catastrophe hits or a disease robs us of our good health and we're in the throes of a serious confrontation. Is the end near for us, or a loved one?

Our character type determines our behavior. A backstory is key to reflect upon and fill in the blanks so we can see how our scene plays out. Is there resignation or regret?

A doctor can be too general if you're not careful. Don't create a cardboard cutout. Define the specific traits of your role and connect to the need of the patient. Reflect upon your history with the healthy patient who is free of a life-threatening disease. Examine that contrast.

Sincere, real, heartfelt emotions must be unearthed. Anything short of this is unacceptable. Personalize your part to add extra drama. Make it intense and urgent.

Last Words

It's funny how you live your whole life wanting all the wrong things, but you don't realize it until you're flat on your back in a hospital bed. All I wanted was money. The more I had, the more I wanted. I never treated you or the kids right. I missed every school play, and just bought you things to make up for all those big business trips. What good is it to me now? I lost half of it in the market anyway. I'm sorry I wasn't there when your mother died. I wish the kids were here. They'll never get on a plane fast enough. Just tell them I love them, and please forgive me. Promise me you'll make it up to them, so I can go in peace.

Too Soon

What are you saying? You can't operate? It's too late? That can't be. I won't accept it. I'm not ready. I'm too young. I haven't finished everything. There's so much more I wanted to do. This isn't happening. You can't tell me it is. There has to be another solution. I'll find it. I will. Why are you looking at me like that? Stop giving me that "God have mercy" face. You're not supposed to pity me. You're supposed to see me as another patient you're going to cure. Don't give up on me. I've lived a good life, and I don't deserve this (Stops for a beat). What am I saying? You're just a messenger. I can't blame you. So, this is it, isn't it?

Doctor's Last Call

Mrs. Black? We've tried everything. The tests came back, and there's no change. The new drugs aren't shrinking the tumor, and we can't operate. We want you to be comfortable now. Hospice is ready to come in whenever you want them. Let us know. I'm sorry we didn't catch it earlier. You didn't do anything wrong. It was too small to see in a checkup and it's a rare disease we've never seen. Sometimes science isn't the only answer. I know you have faith, so pray and find peace. If you need any more morphine, let me know. I never want my patients to suffer.

SPY GAMES

What's that behind your back? Are you hiding something from me? Intrigue and dark secrets fascinate us. Guns and gadgets look like child's play, and there's always been something sexy about it all. We fantasize that we're eluding the enemy.

Watch out! There's danger at every turn, so your senses are heightened. The hairs on the back of your neck stand up. Your character thrives on this, but why? Find something in your past that makes you relish this cloak-and-dagger world. Does the enemy have a personal connection to you? Did you stumble into this line of work?

Be observant. Spies are very keen on seeing every detail unfold in scenes. In fact a good actor should be a full-time spy anyway. You need to be watching and learning about life all the time.

Once again, just don't pull the trigger and go right to a James Bond–type character. Create your own unique role. Remember actors must forge fresh templates to excite audiences.

Trapped Below

Don't touch that. It's gonna blow. Look at the inscription at the base. It's the code they had on the blueprint. That's why they sent us here. They thought we'd trigger the warhead and wipe out the White House. Hold it. Did you hear that? Choppers overhead—listen! Are they our guys? Wait a minute. Grab your phone. Type in the security code for Cobra Ops and see if they bite. If they do, we'd better head out. What's the code? What do you mean? (Aims gun.) Oh so that's why you brought me here—it's a setup! Drop the gun or I'll blow your head off. That's it, nice and easy (taps phone). Carrie? Can you hear me? I need backup—now!

Seductress Spy

Why should a big man like you need a bodyguard? You're so strong and capable. I feel safe at least. Can't find many men like you anymore. That was a long plane ride. You must be tired. Let me help you feel better. You don't need that heavy jacket. I know you must be exhausted. I'll help ease those pains. Relax, have a drink. I know just what you need to sleep. Trust me. You look worried—don't fret. I'm not the kind of girl you can't trust. I want to please a man. I know how to make a man like you feel at home. Just lie back. That's it. Close your eyes. Isn't that better? Now let me massage your muscles a bit so you can drift off to dreamland. (Takes out gun, aims.)

MELODRAMAS: SOAP OPERAS AND REALITY TV

"You slept with my boyfriend."

"He just tried to kill me!"

Life is grand in the melodrama. Slights lead to fast actions. The slap on reality TV can be more like a smoking gun in the soap operas.

Somewhere along the line, a woman is cheated out of something and wants payback, whether it's a heightened fight or murder. Soap opera stories have twists and turns that connect and destroy communities, while romance, betrayals, and dark secrets change the fabric of the characters' lives.

Watch out! Don't lose your core beliefs and needs! Soaps are easy to mimic, but go beyond that kind of characterization and focus on the triggers that make you do the dastardly deeds.

Reality TV, as stated before, has a selective casting process like narrative television. It's not pure documentary. These people are picked from a pool of candidates because of their story or personality. These types are acting out for the camera. They are rewarded for their outrageous behavior constantly.

However, also consider how overwhelming it can be to be thrust into the limelight. Suddenly your friends may be jealous, your ego is bloated, and your life is turned upside down. Unlike a trained actor, you don't have technique—you just have this one shot to stand out like a game show contestant. The pressure is on. Therefore, you're in a tenuous position to perform brilliantly or lose your lucrative spot. Uncover the core needs of your character and put that at the base of your work.

Prosecuting Lawyer

You want the court to believe you didn't plot to kill her, even though she was your first wife who betrayed you? She called the cops on you more than once, and then slept with your best friend before seducing you to come back to her to father your two sons, who now wait to find out your fate while they stay in the court's custody. The truth is, no one in your family can be trusted. But one thing is true. You still love her, and you couldn't bear to see her with yet another man. So you waited outside her house to watch her die. Only, she was on to you, and got a private eye to watch your every move. You thought you could outsmart her, so you hired a hit man. Isn't that right?

Mix Up

He's not my brother—he's my son! All this time I didn't know. The nurse switched the babies because Torrence Crown paid her. My brother has been missing for all these years, but I'll find him. I just heard that Crown's held a grudge because my father filed that lawsuit that broke up all the land between Crown's sons. I think my brother is working on one of their estates. He's maybe been held hostage all of these years, against his will. I got a PI to trail every one of those rotten brothers. They think they can throw me off with all that paperwork down at the courthouse? That phony birth certificate—ha! They will find out just how the Fontaine family gets justice very soon!

Catfight Reality

She started it. She said I was too fat to be with Danny, and too old. I mean, really? Look at her. She's barely able to squeeze into that dress. Yeah, that's right. Come at me. I'll scratch your eyes out. I've been hurt before but I've been shamed for the last time by your gossip. She spreads lies all over the town, and my kids hear it too. Don't smirk at me. I'll slap that face. You know I'm right. Everyone in the house agreed, we'd spend the week away from our families and reconnect—but she was trouble from the start because I was everybody's favorite, and she couldn't stand it. Gotta feel sorry for her, I guess, but I'm not going to take it from her. So look out, Tammy, I'm protecting my family now!

IMPROV EXERCISES FOR WEBISODE CHALLENGES

You may be asked to pitch in on webisodes or independent projects as an actor. If you know your character, you should be able to jump right in, but remember you're also working with others. Share the creative space, so to speak.

Here are some exercises to play with to stimulate your imagination so that you're ready to go with the flow when needed.

Finish the Story

Take a play that you're working on and add another monologue at the end for your character.

If you're working with a scene partner, improvise the scene that follows that last scene or fast-forward to a time in the future and create a scene.

You can also watch your favorite TV show and do a monologue for a character you know after the episode is over. Figure out what happens next and improvise it.

Again, if you're with a group of actors, watch and then do the next scene of a TV program. This could also be done on stage for an improv show, but you'd have a narrator describe the previous scene and then players would jump in and do the following scene.

Problem Solving

The scriptwriter just got a high-paying gig and isn't coming to the set today, so now you have to come up with the first scene of the webisode with the other players.

Watch webisodes to become familiar with different styles. Read over plot synopses for webisodes. Select a synopsis and use it to create a monologue for the first scene of the episode. You can also work with other actors and improvise an opening scene.

Then study a series of webisodes and imagine what the next one would be. Improvise a monologue that would be in the episode. Then watch the produced webisode and see how the scene was filmed. You can also do the aforementioned exercise and stop at various places in the series to explore different stages of plot development.

Play with Situations

It is said that nothing is stranger than truth, so use that for inspiration. Watch news clips of real people facing a range of scenarios. Do a pre-interview monologue for an interviewee as if you are talking to the reporter prior to the news report.

Watch real-life scenes unfold at the mall or public place. Go home and improvise how each character plays out their next scene. Reenact both parts for fun.

Also, do a monologue for each character. Make your speech about what you imagine you'd really want from your friend, family member, or acquaintance.

Study the Play Unfolding

Here's a passive character study. Observe people throughout the week and figure out how they react to different situations. Watch how someone goes crazy over a tiny thing or is totally calm in a life-threatening moment. Make note of how each character vies for what they want and how events trigger responses.

Personal Improv Exercises

How does your scene unfold? Play with pretend scenarios and create reactions you would make in the following situations. Act it out with movement. Imagine who you would talk to and what you would do in these instances. You don't have to play the other participants' parts, just imagine you're hearing what they say and react. You can also create monologues recounting these situations and figure out who you would tell these stories to and why.

Here are the events to use for this exercise:

—Your house has been robbed.

—You saw a mouse.

—You just won $100.

—The dog up the street was just hit by a car.

—You got the wrong coffee at your favorite shop.

—The movie is sold out.

—It's the last play and your favorite team is going to the series.

—Your lover walked in on you cheating.

—You see the boss doing something you can use against him, and he spots you.

—You see the meter maid give you a ticket.

—Your agent called and you booked a series.

—Your play was cancelled.

—The World Trade Towers collapsed.

—Your mother-in-law wants to stay the week.

—Your pet needs surgery—again.

—There's a two-for-one sale, but you have your acting class.

—Your sibling or friend was in an accident.

—Your child got straight As.

—A rock band moved next door and you have a five AM call time.

—Someone just yelled inappropriately at your kid at the sporting event.

—You're fired.

—You've won the lottery for a million dollars.

—Your best friend from high school was named head of a production studio.

—There's an earthquake.

—A new ice cream store opened and there are free samples.

—Your acting teacher tells you that you'll never make it.

—You happen upon a litter of adorable kittens.

—Your parents are moving next door.

—Your friend got free tickets to your favorite show.

—You've just been evicted.

—You got a big bonus in your paycheck.

—Spielberg called back.

12

Monologues and Acting Sides

The following scenes and monologues cover a range of genres—you'll find theater, webisodes, TV, and commercial scripts. In some instances, there will be no specific scene or character descriptions because you can locate those clues easily in the material. A variety of writers have contributed the scripts, so you can experiment with different writing styles. You will be given background information for scenes when necessary, and all scripts will have study notes for you to explore for each scenario.

STUDY GUIDE FOR *HOMEWORK* WRITTEN BY BONNIE MACBIRD (COPYRIGHT © 2009 BONNIE MACBIRD)

Scene: Coworkers redefine their relationship when they are confined in an elevator after a holiday break.

Characters: You should have a good sense of who Katie and Jamie are from the information in the script.

INT. LARGE COMPANY ELEVATOR - EARLY MORNING

Crowded with 6-7 OFFICE WORKERS, snow dusting winter coats.
Silence. In front is KATIE PETERSEN, 28, adorable, slightly
frumpy, big coat, an odd hat. Fighting tears.

Elevator stops, a couple of people get off. JAMIE HERNANDEZ,
30, handsome, disheveled, in wrinkled shirtsleeves, loosened
tie, and thin sheen of sweat, gets on. He spots Katie and
edges past two bundled office types to stand next to her.

                    JAMIE
          'Scuse me. 'Scuse...
             (sotto voce)
          Hey Katie. It's Katie, right, from
          Contracts?

                    KATIE
          Oh. Uh… yeah…

                    JAMIE
          I almost didn't recognize you in
          that hat. That's a panda bear,
          right?

                    KATIE
          Penguin. Penguin with glasses.

                    JAMIE
          Chanukah present?

                    KATIE
          Christmas.

                    JAMIE
          0 for 2.

He grins at the other passengers who do not react. She faces
front resolutely trying to avoid further contact. A beat.

                    JAMIE
          I like penguins. Did you go away
          for the holidays?

She stifles a sob, then looks away..

                    JAMIE
          I had to work through. Twelve
          sneaks on the new Matt Damon flick
          - I was up all night doing the
          report. I could use a shower.
          Excuse me, everybody.

KATIE looks away, wishing she were not standing next to him.

                    JAMIE (CONT'D)
            So it looks like the flick is big
            with chicks over 35… if you still
            call them chicks at that age.

                    KATIE
            Look, I forget your first name.
            But discretion is maybe not your
            middle name.

                    JAMIE
            Jamie. Jamie "Discretion"
            Hernandez down in Marketing
            Research. We danced at the holiday
            party?

Katie stares blankly.

                    JAMIE
            I stepped on your foot. How is it
            by the way?

                    KATIE
            Oh my god, you! Get away from me.

                    JAMIE
            It still hurts? Look, I'm sorry. I-

The bell DINGS and everyone else on the elevator rushes off.
Katie pauses a beat, decides she's safest if she gets off,
too. Moves toward the door but Jamie blocks her way.

                    KATIE
            Will you please move?

                    JAMIE
            This isn't your floor.

                    KATIE
            It probably isn't anyone's floor.
            We just want to get away from YOU.

                    JAMIE
            Katie, please. Give me a second.

                    KATIE
            No! If you'd just -

                    JAMIE
            I wanted to ask you out. Again.
            But I can see that you're upset.

                    KATIE
            Well, yeah! You're upsetting me -

                        JAMIE
          No, before. Kinda teary. Bad
          holidays?

                        KATIE
          Those weren't tears; they were,you
          know, eyes watering from the cold.
          Outside.

The elevator doors have closed. Elevator moves. DINGS. Door
opens.

                        JAMIE
          Here you are! The story department!

He places a hand in the small of her back as if to guide her
out the door.

                        KATIE
          Take your hand off me right now.

JAMIE removes his hand, fast.

                        JAMIE
          Okay,okay. No hands.
               (holds hands up)
          No tricks up my sleeves. No
          ulterior motives or sneaky plots.
          Although I'm sure they -
               (nods to story department)
          -could write us a "cute meet" for
          our first date.

The elevator door closes. Jamie glances behind Katie.

                        JAMIE (CONT'D)
          Hey! Is that an earring?

As she turns to look, he hits a button on the panel. The
elevator stops.

                        JAMIE (CONT'D)
          Oops, it's just a piece of tinsel.

                        KATIE
          Get this. I am not in the dating
          market. Period.

                        JAMIE
          I don't see a ring.

                        KATIE
          Why isn't this elevator moving?

                    JAMIE
          Are you secretly married? Gay?
          Because if you are, it's okay - I
          think -

                    KATIE
          Not married. Not gay. Why isn't
          this button lighting up?

                    JAMIE
          You do not have the look of a woman
          in love.

                    KATIE
          What is the MATTER WITH THIS
          ELEVATOR? We are NOT MOVING.

                    JAMIE
          I found your blog over Christmas.

KATIE looks at him in sudden horror.

                    KATIE
          Oh, my God, no!

                    JAMIE
          And I read it. You are one
          insanely hot chick.

Katie can't help a quick grin of pleasure, which she quickly
tries to hide. He hits a button the elevator starts to move.

                    KATIE
          No. You're bluffing. I use a
          pseudonym. There's no way -

                    JAMIE
          That's right, I'm bluffing. But I
          will read it now. I'm Jamie
          Indiscretion Hernandez, research
          king. I can find anything on the
          internet. And I will find you.

The elevator arrives and doors open. He turns to her with a
smile.

                    JAMIE
          Never underestimate the power of a
          man who does his homework!

He exits. The door shuts. Katie pauses, alone in the
elevator. Slowly a broad grin steals over her face.

Some Evident Clues for Your Characters

—You work at an office.

—Work has commenced after the holidays.

—There was an office party prior to your break.

—You danced with someone from the office at the party.

⬚ Dig deeper for more evident truths.

Questions to Explore for Jamie

How long have you been admiring Katie?

Did she come on to you at the party, or did you take advantage of her?

What's it like spending the holidays working most of the time?

Since you're a researcher, are you a people person?

How high are the stakes for you to connect with Katie now?

Are you popular or not invited to social affairs?

Questions to Explore for Katie

How difficult is it for you to cry in public?

What makes you want to cry right now?

What happened that prompted you to let Jamie dance with you at the party?

How have boyfriends treated you in the past?

Why does the sudden attention with the blog break the ice?

Are you a wannabe writer or a writer?

What specifically makes you smile about what Jamie says?

Scene Considerations

This is a romantic scene with universal themes. Each character wants to be loved. Katie is vulnerable. Both characters are worn down by current circumstances. Katie is distraught and Jamie has worked all night. Being trapped in an elevator forces Katie to communicate and let her guard down. Jamie sees his opportunity and pounces.

Fun Ideas

Switch parts to figure out which character matches your type most. Experiment with different settings or age ranges that might be closer to what you might play. For example, you could be two coeds coming back from break. Perhaps you had danced at a campus party before the holiday.

STUDY GUIDE FOR *KITTEN RESCUE–HOMELESS* WRITTEN BY SHARI BECKER

Style: This is a commercial script, so make sure you adhere to this genre.

Some Evident Clues

Wild cats are at risk of getting pregnant.
A life on the street can be dangerous for an animal.
More unwanted kittens might be born and need to be rescued.

Elements to Explore

—Take the time to build the reality of the scene and see very specific details.
—Don't take a maudlin approach for this. Devise a lot of levels and beats.
—Imagine the settings of the alley and the abandoned house to make your scene come alive. Do an improvisation where you witness the helpless kittens in these scenes.
—Tell it to someone you know well and focus on their reactions, making good use of a Meisner technique.
—Remember, you are doing something good by sharing this information and find the joy in that.

Experiment

You can do this as if it were for a voice-over instead. Rely on your imagination to visualize the commercial and to connect to the scenes. Don't read it, you still have to tell it to one person for a very important reason.

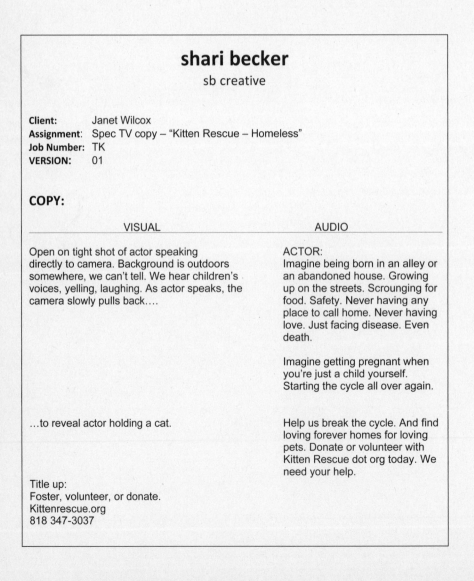

shari becker
sb creative

Client: Janet Wilcox
Assignment: Spec TV copy – "Kitten Rescue – Homeless"
Job Number: TK
VERSION: 01

COPY:

VISUAL	AUDIO
Open on tight shot of actor speaking directly to camera. Background is outdoors somewhere, we can't tell. We hear children's voices, yelling, laughing. As actor speaks, the camera slowly pulls back….	ACTOR: Imagine being born in an alley or an abandoned house. Growing up on the streets. Scrounging for food. Safety. Never having any place to call home. Never having love. Just facing disease. Even death.

Imagine getting pregnant when you're just a child yourself. Starting the cycle all over again. |
| …to reveal actor holding a cat. | Help us break the cycle. And find loving forever homes for loving pets. Donate or volunteer with Kitten Rescue dot org today. We need your help. |
| Title up: Foster, volunteer, or donate. Kittenrescue.org 818 347-3037 | |

Monologue from "**My Audition for Almodovar**"

by **Alberto Ferreras**

Premiered at Teatro IATI, New York City, July 2010
Starring Inma Heredia

This is an interactive comedy monologue written for an
actress who speaks with a thick Spanish accent. It could be
adapted for other genders and/or nationalities.

***

**Actor should engage the
audience directly, making eye
contact with them, in the
same way a teacher would
stand in front of a class.**

I don't know if you have noticed but… I have a little bit
of an accent. Yes, I know, it's barely noticeable, but it
happens to those of us who learned English later in life.
No matter how hard we try, we all end up speaking with an
accent.

Oh, but don't get me wrong, my accent doesn't bother me at
all. I actually love my accent! I think that my accent is
part of my charm. The problem is that there are certain
directors and producers out there who don't seem to
appreciate it.

I have many friends—fellow actors from Puerto Rico and Mexico—who always complain that the only parts they get are drug-dealers and prostitutes. But with my Spanish accent I can not even get those parts. What do they think, that there are no drug-dealers and prostitutes in Spain? Hello???

The problem is that, in Hollywood, they only make <u>one</u> part a year for an actor with my accent, and if they can't give it to Antonio Banderas then—without a doubt—they will give it to the despicable, the unbearable… Penelope Cruz! Ugh! I can't stand Penelope Cruz! Am I the only one here who hates her?

The moment I hear that name my blood starts boiling, and I just want to… I just want to…

APPROACHING SOMEONE FROM THE AUDIENCE

Excuse me, would you mind if we pretend that you are Penelope Cruz? Just so I can focus my anger. I'm not going to hurt you—I promise—I just need a spot where I can go…

TURNING VIOLENT TOWARDS

PENELOPE

Grrrrr!!! I hate you!!! I hate you!!! I hate you!!!

CALMING DOWN

Wow! I'm feeling better already. Thank you dear.

BACK TO THE AUDIENCE

See… if Penelope was in Spain, I wouldn't care…
She could live happily ever after making movies, selling
make up, or stepping on grapes. She would be happy, I would
be happy… But no, she had to come here to manipulate, to
monopolize, to take that <u>one</u> part that opens up <u>once</u> a year
for an actress like <u>me</u>.

ANGRY AGAIN, TO PENELOPE

I HATE YOU!!!!!!

CALMING DOWN, TO PENELOPE

Thank you dear.

BACK TO THE AUDIENCE

And correct me if I'm wrong but her looks are nothing to write home about, her acting skills are so-so, and her accent is totally fake… I mean, I'm a starving actress, I work in The Bronx and live in Washington Heights, I can <u>not</u> afford to get rid of my accent… but Penelope???

TO PENELOPE

Come on! Don't tell me that you can't afford a speech coach!!! Shame on you!!!

BACK TO AUDIENCE

But don't let my accent fool you. I'll have you know that I happen to have a Masters Degree in English Literature. Yes, it's from a university that you've never heard of, but I have it! I've read William Shakespeare, James Joyce, Danielle Steel… I've read them all. I'm telling you, I speak English very well! The only problem is… my accent.

And forgive me for sidetracking but now that we're talking about studies, we need to talk about one more thing that pisses me off: I hate when people say that they don't speak Spanish, that they speak Castilian. Haven't you heard that?

"Oh, I don't speak Spanish, I speak Castilian"

Yeah, like I'm better than you, because I speak with a lisp. Well, I am *appalled* by their ignorance.

First, let's present the cold facts: Back in the 1400's, Spain was divided in separate regions, and every region had a different language: the Galicians spoke Galician, the Catalunyans spoke Catalunyan, the Valencians spoke Valencian, and obviously the Castilians spoke Castilian.

So in comes this lady, Queen Isabel of Castile, who unified all the kingdoms of the peninsula, and that's how Castilian ended up spreading out throughout the country, and transforming itself into the language that we now call **Spanish**.

That's why we have a **Royal Academy of the *Spanish* Language**, not a **Royal Academy of the *Castilian* Language**. And I'm sorry for bothering you with all this, but I think it's important to educate people, okay? And what drives me nuts, is that some people think that those who speak Spanish in *a certain way* are better than those who speak it in *a different way*. Let's face it: It doesn't matter where you're from, it's what you <u>do</u> that makes you a better person—I think.

So the next time that somebody tells you: "Oh! I don't speak Spanish, I speak Castilian" you can tell them—on my behalf—that they can go to hell!

***

©Alberto Ferreras, 2009

STUDY GUIDE FOR *MY AUDITION FOR ALMODOVAR* WRITTEN BY ALBERTO FERRERAS

The author has given you a lot of clear clues as to who this character is and what the scene is about. You will have to make choices about why it is important for you to share this information.

This is a great monologue to treat as a scenario with multiple scene partners because there are times when you will audition with a side that requires you to speak to different characters. In this instance, you must have specific focal points on the fourth wall space in front of you to see each of the imagined scene partners.

You need to place your partners on a fixed spot to keep all of the characters straight as you bounce between them. You also need to call on very detailed images of what the person looks like, so you clearly demonstrate that you are speaking to a real person. Pick appropriate friends from your own life to make it more personal and natural.

In regard to gender, you can switch Antonio Banderas for Penélope Cruz if you are a male actor. Simply modify some of the descriptions to match the masculine character.

This has a lot of humor in it, but don't push for the laughs, be sincere. Your character is an actor who wants to work and you are frustrated. Come up with some very unique reasons this is important to you now. Think of your life and how you are treated like a second-class citizen at times.

Whether you have an authentic accent or not, personalize this so that you have a strong *as if* to translate this into your life. For example, as a woman, I had to fight to get directing opportunities when I started my career. Use something real, and emotionally charged, in your own life.

Practice this as an intimate scene in a small room for contrast so you don't do it too broad. Make your emotional choices real, justified, and painful.

Don't forget pacing and timing. These elements make or break the success of a comedic monologue. Delve into different levels and beats—don't make this flat or one note. Do a scale of emotions throughout the piece as you rehearse to unearth new moments.

If you are substituting an accent that is not Spanish, adapt the writing to work with your dialect choice. You could use a Southern or British actor, for example; just end your monologue prior to the Castilian section. Experiment with this. Think of an actor who seems to take all your parts and substitute that name into the script and modify the material. In fact, it may be very funny to select an actor very far from your type and explore that. Whatever you decide, find real meaningful reasons why you have to say this and know specifically what you want from your scene partners.

SPECIAL CONSIDERATIONS FOR THE FOLLOWING SCRIPT

Do this monologue two ways. First, practice a shorter version of it. Start the soliloquy at the fifth paragraph with the sentence beginning with "We got to this point . . ."

Rehearse the abbreviated version. Make choices based only on this portion of the script. Then look at the whole script and see what you may have overlooked. If you haven't performed longer monologues, this will help raise the bar for you.

From "Paterfamilias," by Susan Bullington Katz

Mags is somewhere in her
40's, pretty, who once
tried her hand at glamour
and has settled into a
softer wholesomeness
instead.
Jilly is her younger
sister.
They've been going through
boxes of mementoes in Mags'
house, and Jilly has asked
her about a man in a
photograph.

MAGS

We did go out walking once. You know, he couldn't
see, but I thought maybe I could help him. Maybe I
could, and we would stay on the trail and it
would... well, wouldn't it be exhilarating for him
and me, too, to be up on that trail that starts at
the base of Sunset Blvd., right near the nursery
there, and winds up to the ridge of the Santa
Monica mountains, and then follows the crest of the
hill?

You can see - that is, if you can see - but he
could see shapes and things, and I think he knew
the water was there, even if he couldn't see each
little whitecap of each little wave - you're
walking on the ridge of these mountains and you can
see downtown L.A. on one side and the Pacific Ocean
on the other. I mean, there it is, in full color,
some cinematographer's dream.

So to get up there, I fixed my backpack with four bottles of water - two apiece - and four granola bars - this was before the advent of Balance bars - and he had brought his cane. I thought I would watch for roots for two. So we went. Slowly. We went, and he was so excited that I wanted to do this - more excited, I think, about my wanting to do it than about doing it, but he did it - he went along, and we're out there, and people scrambling up the trail all around us - people, dogs, kids - and there was this moment when we were halfway up to the top, and it wasn't really easy because I had to assume this mommy role - this role of pathfinder - telling him where to step and what to avoid, and "Don't put your foot down there - there's a big place where the path has washed away!" So it wasn't really fun, but it was an experiment, you know. To see if we could do this.

The two of us. Together.

We got to this point, a stopping-off place where people went out on the ledge to scope out the view. And I was guiding him over toward it, and all the people were in the background, and I realized how distinguished he looked. His white hair just straggly enough that it was flowing a little in the breeze. Just a little. And his cane. And the way he held himself. Like he remembered, always, the line-up of cases he had won, and the causes he had fought for. And then I looked more closely, and there, in the bright sunlight, out in the wind, I realized he looked... old. Old and fragile. And that was when I realized that I couldn't do it. Couldn't go beyond there with him.

Because it wasn't about him, Jilly. It was about
me. Me feeling old and fragile. And looking at him
reminded me of that. And I had just buried one
marriage. I didn't want to have found a new man, a
good one, and have him die on me, too.
So I climbed to the top of the hill. He made it,
all the way, but at the top, when the really
appropriate thing to do would have been to hug him
out of the exhilaration of having gotten to the
top, all I wanted to do was head back down again,
the sooner to get to the part where I would take
him to the airport, kiss him goodbye, and turn him
into a memory.

STUDY GUIDE FOR *PATERFAMILIAS* WRITTEN BY SUSAN BULLINGTON KATZ (COPYRIGHT © 2010 SBK)

The author has given you a brief character and scene description. Use it as you work on the whole the monologue.

Evident Clues

—Two sisters are going through mementos and it triggers memories for the older sister, Mags.

—Mags recalls helping an older visually impaired man walk up a daunting hill.

—The two start the climb at the base of Sunset Blvd.

▶ Dig deeper for more evident truths.

Questions to Explore for Mags

Why are the sisters going through the boxes?

Did Mags become interested in this man on the rebound from a previous relationship?

Does she like playing a nurturing role to him?

What was Mags looking for in him—a father figure, provider, or soul mate?

Does Mags have any regret or guilt as she tells this story?

Why is it important for the relationship to work for Mags as she begins the climb?

As they pause on the hill, she takes time to reflect about her life. Is this the first time she accepts the finality of her previous marriage?

The light is a trigger for Mags to see the man differently. Why did Mags fail to see things clearly before?

How did these two meet? What was good about their relationship? Climbing the mountain is like a rite of passage on to a new stage of life for Mags. Does she realize she wants to live in the present again?

CHALLENGES FOR THE FOLLOWING SCRIPT

Repeat the same process outlined with the previous script. First, rehearse a shorter version of this script. Begin at the ninth paragraph with the sentence starting with "So you got your degree . . ."

Practice this shorter segment and then look at the whole script. Make note of your right and wrong choices. Use the long monologue as a workout challenge for your focus and concentration.

STUDY GUIDE FOR *THE NOZZLE MAN* WRITTEN BY JOHN BROSNAN

The author provides detailed information about your scene. Proceed to work on the whole script after you have experimented with the aforementioned abbreviated section.

Some Evident Clues

—A nephew and uncle are having drinks.
—The uncle fights fires in the Bronx.
—He's a nozzle man who is closest to the fire.
—He is forced to retire due to health problems.
—His nephew is considering joining the force.
▶ Probe deeper for more clues.

"The Nozzle Man"
By John Brosnan

MIKE "SPARKY" MULVAHILL, 45, six foot and change.
Firefighting isn't his "job," it is his life. He's
a stand-up guy and the type of New Yorker who'd
give you the shirt off his back without blinking.
In a typical Brooklyn bar, he sits with his nephew
CHRIS MULVAHILL, 25, a bright, blue collar kid
standing at the crossroads of his adult life. He
wears an "N.Y.U." sweatshirt.

MIKE

So you wanted to know about the job, kid…? You old
enough to drink? You just graduated, right? So I
guess you are. Pete, give us a couple of Harps over
here when you get a chance, okay?

The job… I was always in it for the action, for the
firefighting… Some guys went to firehouses in
Manhattan for the chicks. Me, I wanted the busiest
firehouse in the city. Don't get me wrong, chicks
were always a great perk, but they didn't feed that
part of me … the part that needed to fight fires.
I'm no pyro, but I love fire. It's a beautiful and
dangerous thing and there's nothing like subduing
it with your guys, your gear and your guts.

As a kid, my Dad, your Grandfather --- God-rest-
his-soul --- had a scanner and he'd listen for fire

calls. When he heard one, he'd throw us kids into the car --- it was one of those wagons with the wood on the sides --- and we'd speed off to watch the firemen puttin' out fires. Looking back, I guess it was crazy, but we loved it. Watching the action was probably the only thing that could keep us kids from fighting each other.

Now, not to be fighting, that was an unnatural state for me… As a kid, I had thick, Coke bottle glasses, like Froggy from "The Little Rascals"…not the originals, but the later ones, "Our Gang," which sucked. Kids were always trying to talk shit to me 'cause of my glasses. Glasses or not, I was not the shit-taking type so I got into fights. Lots of 'em, even after I got contacts… Can't remember when the fights stopped. Probably when I joined the Fire Department. Then again, ha, maybe not…

So yeah, I wanted to fight fires, kid. And man, I got what I wanted and then some. The yearly average for a New York City firehouse is about two, three thousand calls. We ran five thousand calls a year. Sometimes more. That made ours the busiest firehouse in the city, maybe the world, kid. That's the Bronx for you: crazy. "The Bronx Zoo" we called it --- junkies, mutts, skells and mopes all around you, but a lot of good people just trying ta live and not get hit with a bucket of steaming crap. And me, hell, I was just tryin' to keep 'em alive, ya know?

You still with me, Chris? So the bell goes off, you pull your gear --- you done it a million times, it's like a second skin: boots, pants, helmet, turnout coat, Scott pack, radio, your tools, everything. It's a lot, but you got it on in seconds --- you don't even think about it. You jump on the truck run lights and sirens to the scene. Your heart's pumpin' like a Hunts Point whore because you don't know what to expect. Then the truck pulls up to the scene and "BOOM-BOOM!" the Captain bangs on the door of the rig. That's the signal: "Get your asses out of the engine, you're about to get hot." Your heart rate jumps a couple'a gears as you head into that burning structure. It's not natural to want to go into a building on fire, but it's what you do, so you go right in with your crew.

In the fire, when I'm the "nozzle man," I'm the rock star of the crew. You're up front, closest to the fire, the heat and all that. It's my job to put the water on the fire to knock it down. So the heat is on you, not just from the fire, but from your crew --- you gotta keep your head, move forward, get the job done. Otherwise, people, including your fellow firefighters, might get hurt. If you screw the pooch, you are in for some serious ball-breaking by your crew. Hopefully, that's the worst of it. You gotta love it, and it's the best place ta be in a fire --- front row seat. Chris, I known you since before you was born. And I know firemen of all types for many years. You, you got enough balls and brains ta make a good "nozzle man," kid.

But things always change, even when they shouldn't.
College boys're running the fire department now.
Lots of new rules. Rules that don't always make
sense to a fireman. Now, I got nothing against
people who went to college --- look at you --- but
these jokers, they like to make changes for no real
reason, just because they can. So now a guy has ta
have a college degree to be a New York City
fireman?!! I mean, what the hell is that…?!! No
offense, kid, but this is the best fire department
in the world and it was built mostly by blue-collar
guys…guys like me. None of us had college degrees
and we didn't need 'em to be the best at this job.
Why some dumbass bureaucrat who never got picked on
the playground would toss guys like me out the
window escapes me, but I guess that's above my pay
grade.

So…you got your degree and that's great, kid.
You're a smart guy, Christopher. It'll open a lot
of doors. You want to make money…crazy money? Then
take that degree straight to Wall Street. You can
do that and lose your soul at the same time. But if
you want to save lives, bust your ass, work with
great guys and do a job that most people fear…?
Then be a firefighter, kid. Best thing I ever
done…and I'll sure as hell miss it.

Ya know, I envy you, kid, I really do. You got it
all in front of you. Me, I'm done. Retiring. Yeah,
that's right. After I got out of the hospital, I
went down to Lafayette Street to get checked out.
The Doc said, "You're done. Too broken down. You're

a liability to the City." Imagine that. After all
those years, all those fires? A "liability"?
I never, ever expected it to end for me, kid.
Thought I'd be fighting fires up in the Bronx 'til
the day I died. Now I don't know what I'm gonna
do…it's a part of me, like my lungs, my eyes or my
soul.

But you…? Chris, you got it all in front of you.
You can do anything. Whatever you want! Just one
thing I need you to do for me, kid: if you go into
the Department, don't tell your Mom we talked… My
sister'll throw a beating on me worse than that
damned fire. Know that I'm sayin'?

Scene Considerations

Be careful not to do a clichéd accent for Mike. Make his life real and accessible. Practice it without an accent if you have trouble at first. Then study the accent and layer it onto your work later. Find a strong dangerous substitution for the love of fire—we all do risky things. Also consider all of the good things you do in your life that can be an *as if* for saving lives.

Questions to Explore for Mike

How close are you to your nephew?

Do you think your nephew could be a firefighter?

What do you lose if you don't convince him that this is a great career? Is he the son you never had? Will he keep you connected vicariously to that life?

How close are you to your sister? Explore the roles you play in the family.

This scene deals with the past, present, and future. You represent the past and your nephew represents the future. What is there in the present?

How can such a tough guy be so afraid of the world outside of firefighting?

Why do educated newcomers threaten you? Were you a bad student?

Is your poor health a sign of losing the masculine façade you cling to, and how do you cope with that?

INTRODUCTION TO *THE MILE-HIGH CLUB* WRITTEN BY ROSANNE WELCH

The following three scenes are from *The Mile-High Club* script. The Mile-High Diner is nestled in a National Forest region patrolled by park rangers. Locals often convene at the diner to drink, eat, and gab.

Aunt Joanne owns the diner and has employed her thirty-six-year-old niece, Kathy, to help her. Kathy recently left her abusive husband, Rick, and has moved here with her two boys, Michael and Robert.

A news report reveals that a bullet-riddled car has been found in the local area. Dean, a ranger, has caught Kathy's son Bobby with a girl drinking forbidden alcohol in the forest. While Bobby is working off the fine for Dean, they find a bear feasting on the body of a teenager who was in the car. Kathy's parental authority is diminished after Bobby happens upon Kathy and Gerry, a young park ranger, sleeping together on the couch. To make matters worse, Bobby's father, Rick, comes to town in this time of crisis.

                          ACT THREE

FADE IN:

INT. DINER — NIGHT

Gerry and Freddie sit at the bar, nursing coffee mugs since
they're both now on duty in the wake of this find. The joint
is definitely jumping with looky-loos watching both the
television -- and the regulars reaction to the story.

                    NEWS ANCHOR
            Mrs. Carney went into seclusion on
            hearing the news. Police are still
            interviewing the park ranger who
            made the discovery. No footage is
            yet available and the police are not
            releasing the exact location where
            the body was found.

                    GERRY
            Like they should sell the tickets. I've
            already chased off three souvenir
            hunters.

He grabs the remote control and switches it off.

                    AUNT JOANNE
                (dumbfounded)
            He really was the boy in the
            Corvette...

                    GERRY
            That's what the cop told me.

                    FREDDIE
            Poor kid. Rich. Young. Had his
            whole life set.

                    AUNT JOANNE
            Poor Kathy... She was so proud of
            making that boy work off his fine
            with Dean.

                    GERRY
            Sequoia sempervirens.

                    FREDDIE
            Say again?

                    GERRY
            I just... She just wanted Bobby to
            learn to like this place, appreciate
            how different it was from other
            places...

> AUNT JOANNE
Can't hide from the city.

> GERRY
Can't hide from life.

> FREDDIE
Aren't supposed to. Everything
happens for a reason, effects
everything else, whether you know it
or not... Heck, my parents met at a
hanging.

> GERRY
Seriously?

> FREDDIE
At a boarding house in the depression.
Older man couldn't pay up, couldn't
face everyone knowing he failed. So
he strung himself up with the rope
belt he'd been wearing 'cause he
couldn't afford leather. My folks
met in the hallway watching the Irish
cop drag him out in a bag.

> GERRY
And this is relevant because...?

> FREDDIE
I wouldn'ta been around if he hadn't
decided not to be.

> GERRY
So what're we supposed to learn from
this?

(Pondering that, they turn their attention to the door where

DEAN

enters. The crowd quiets down.)

> AUNT JOANNE
Keep your ears to yourself. Nothing
new about a man who knows where to get
a burger rare and a beer cold.

(More folks take her advice)

> AUNT JOANNE (CONT'D)
Where they at?

(Others exit grumpily.)

                        DEAN
            I drove 'em home after we finished
            the paperwork.

                        AUNT JOANNE
            So it's over.

                        DEAN
            Not for Kathy and her boy. Boys.
            Father was waiting for 'em when we
            pulled up.

                        AUNT JOANNE
            Vulture.   ←————————— **End Scene**

EXT. WARREN CABIN — NIGHT

A motorcycle we haven't seen before sits in front. Voices
are raised within -- raised but not shouting. Yet.

INT. WARREN CABIN — NIGHT — LATER

RICK WARREN, 38, a poor man's version of David Lee Roth,
stands toe to toe with Kathy.

                        KATHY
            You can't just feed him a bowl of
            Wheaties and send him to bed. He's
            hurting.

                        RICK
            Can't treat him like a kitten, either.
            He'll get over it.

                        KATHY
            Says you.

                        RICK
            Remember when we saw Marty wipe out
            in Michigan? I got over it.

                        KATHY
            This isn't going to go away after
            one beer—soaked wake. Bobby might
            have to go to court and testify to
            discovering a boy who went from
            cruising to Crunch and Munch in one
            night.

                        RICK
            So much for Mayberry.

                        KATHY
            You act like I knew this would happen.
            Like it was a choice between your
            violent tendencies or the world's.

SCENE ONE CONSIDERATIONS FOR
THE MILE-HIGH CLUB

You may choose a character that has a few lines, but this is a meaty scene. A murder has happened in an idyllic setting. Locals come here for comfort. Think of how levity helps to relieve tension in the scene.

Some Character Notes and Questions

Here are condensed key defining characteristics the author presents in the full pilot for the roles in *The Mile-High Club* scenes.

Freddie Hernandez, sixty-eight, is a regular customer at the diner. He sits at the counter wearing a senior patch on a volunteer forest service uniform shirt. Often, he is the voice of reason when disputes arise and he's a bit of a father figure in Kathy's life.

> What does the diner provide that is missing in his home?
> Why does he want to help Kathy?

Gerry Reubens is a sexy twenty-six-year-old forest ranger. He's a wise guy, but he has genuine feelings for Kathy and her sons.

> Does he represent hope?
> Why is he so eager to help Kathy?

Dean Wakeman, forty-eight, is a modern lone ranger. His uniform is as fastidious as the one he wore in the Special Forces in Vietnam. He brings a tough dose of no-nonsense reality to the group.

> Why is discipline so important for him?
> What pushed him in that direction in life—an unhappy family life? A war?

Aunt Joanne, a cross between Emmylou Harris and Katharine Hepburn, is in her mid to late fifties with long salt-and-pepper hair.

She's the host of the party so to speak, a nurturer, but at the end of the day, how close is she to anyone?

Does Kathy help her heal the wounds of her past?

News Anchor is presented as a general character, so you must make it very specific and real.

Is this a scoop or a usual story?

Are you a vain talent or serious reporter?

Who do you imagine your character is speaking to when you deliver the news?

What draws you to the seamy side of life?

How serious is this death to the community?

How does it alter the everyday lives of the people?

Are the locals more frightened of future deaths?

Rick Warren, thirty-eight, is a poor man's David Lee Roth. He's behind on his child support payment. Rick has abused Kathy in the past and wants to help now, but he doesn't seem to know how to nurture the boys.

Kathy Warren, thirty-six, is a cross between Erin Brockovich and Lorelai Gilmore. She has brought her two sons (Michael, seven, and Robert, thirteen) here to escape her husband's abuse and to start a new life. Kathy is a typical single mother: alone, frightened, and struggling to be strong.

Bobby Warren, thirteen, is dealing with his quarreling parents who are now free to date new partners. He is also exploring his own sexual awakening.

Michael Warren, seven, is sweet and devoted to Kathy. He's recently adopted two baby mice that he found.

                    DEAN
        I drove 'em home after we finished
        the paperwork.

                    AUNT JOANNE
        So it's over.

                    DEAN
        Not for Kathy and her boy. Boys.
        Father was waiting for 'em when we
        pulled up.

                    AUNT JOANNE
        Vulture.

EXT. WARREN CABIN — NIGHT   ⟵————————— **Start Scene**

A motorcycle we haven't seen before sits in front. Voices
are raised within -- raised but not shouting. Yet.

INT. WARREN CABIN — NIGHT — LATER

RICK WARREN, 38, a poor man's version of David Lee Roth,
stands toe to toe with Kathy.

                    KATHY
        You can't just feed him a bowl of
        Wheaties and send him to bed. He's
        hurting.

                    RICK
        Can't treat him like a kitten, either.
        He'll get over it.

                    KATHY
        Says you.

                    RICK
        Remember when we saw Marty wipe out
        in Michigan? I got over it.

                    KATHY
        This isn't going to go away after
        one beer-soaked wake. Bobby might
        have to go to court and testify to
        discovering a boy who went from
        cruising to Crunch and Munch in one
        night.

                    RICK
        So much for Mayberry.

                    KATHY
        You act like I knew this would happen.
        Like it was a choice between your
        violent tendencies or the world's.

                    RICK
        I never hurt the boys.

                    KATHY
        Outside of making them think it's
        okay to hit their women--

                    RICK
        I'm taking the classes.

                    KATHY
        There's a difference between warming
        the chair up to make the judge happy
        and really, actually, trying to be a
        better father.

                    RICK
            (shout)
        I am trying.

                    KATHY
            (shouting back)
        Then why'd it take something like
        this to get you to come see the place
        your sons were living?

                    RICK
            (shouting back again)
        I trusted you.

                    KATHY
            (dead quiet)
        You did?

(He takes a step closer to her)

                    RICK
        Yeah... And maybe I didn't want to
        see the competition. I mean, you've
        got all these trees and space. All
        I've got's a one bedroom with free
        water and satellite TV.

                    KATHY
        Believe it or not they miss your TV
        when they're up here.

(He leans in. Closer. Familiar territory.)

                    RICK
        Yeah?

(Closer.)

                    KATHY
        Yeah.

(And she leans up and kisses him. Hard. He kisses back. No one's reaching for snaps or buttons yet but they are falling back into easy patterns when...)

                    BOBBY
          Shit.

(They turn to find Bobby and Michael in the hallway. Kathy immediately shoves Rick as far away from her as possible.)

                         KATHY
          That's it. I gotta get out of here.

                         RICK
               (eerie...)
          That's what you said when you left
          me.

                         MICHAEL
               (scared)
          You want to leave? Here? Too?

                         BOBBY
          Why? You're the one having all the
          fun.

                         RICK
          Robert.

                         BOBBY
          Don't even try.

                         KATHY
          I know how this looks after last
          night but --

                         BOBBY
          Least you were married to Dad.

(Bobby heads back toward his room. Rick steps in and grabs him by the arm.)

                         RICK
          Don't talk to your mother like that.

                         BOBBY
               (turning on him, too)
          Better I should hit her, huh?

(With that Bobby shakes free and heads to his room.)

                         KATHY
          Great. Now he doesn't have to listen
          to either of us.

(The lock clicks into place on the other side of his bedroom door. The forgotten son speaks up.)

                    MICHAEL
          We can't go without Wilbur.

                    KATHY
          We go when I say we go.

                    MICHAEL
          Freddie said it'd be a couple days
          before he could travel --

                    KATHY
          Not now, Michael.

                    MICHAEL
          He said --

                    KATHY
          Wilbur's dead, Michael. I killed
          him.

(Michael's face freezes.)

                    KATHY (CONT'D)
          I'm sorry. It was an accident.

(Kathy moves to comfort him.)

                    KATHY (CONT'D)
          I tried to make Wilbur better but...

(Michael dodges her arms and hugs Rick. Rick awkwardly hugs
back. Her youngest son finding comfort with her oldest enemy
is the final straw.)

                    KATHY (CONT'D)
          Fine. Take them both. Take it all.

(She walks out to the strains of Tim McGraw's "Angry All the
Time" ("You're not the only one, who feels like this world's
left you far behind... I don't know why you gotta be angry
all the time").

(The door slams shut. Rick doesn't notice,)

BOBBY

(Opens his door at the sound of the front door slamming. He
sees)

MICHAEL

(Hug Rick harder. The look on Rick's face is pure fear.)

BOBBY

(Sees that look. Maybe for the first time...)

SOME EVIDENT CLUES FOR SCENE TWO
OF *THE MILE-HIGH CLUB*

—Two divorcees have to come together for the children.

—The husband has been abusive in the past.

—There is an underlying sexual tension that is present between the couple.

—Their son is in trouble—a crisis must be solved now.

▶ Dig deeper for more evident truths.

Questions to Explore for Kathy

What was Kathy's role in her marriage with Rick (devoted wife, perfectionist, etc.)?

How difficult was it for Kathy to pick up the kids and leave?

What was the final straw that made Kathy leave?

Questions to Explore for Rick

Find the things in the past that led to Rick's abusive behavior. Was he abused?

Does Rick love his children, or does he feel obligated to be here?

What are Rick's dreams and aspirations, and how has life altered them?

Questions to Explore for Bobby

Is he the man of the house without Rick?

Does he feel threatened by Rick?

Is he protective of Kathy or ashamed of her love affair?

Questions to Explore for Michael

Does he turn to Rick for comfort because he feels abandoned by his mom?

Is he frightened when his parents quarrel?

Michael trusted his mom and she let him down. How does he react to that?

OVERVIEW FOR *THE MILE-HIGH CLUB* SCENE THREE

Kathy has just returned after her son Bobby discovered she was kissing his father, Rick. Bobby is in his room with the door closed. He has threatened to leave Kathy and go off to live with Rick. Kathy finds a note from Rick saying he has left. She knocks on Bobby's door determined to find out if he wants to live with her or Rick.

Questions to Explore for Kathy

What are the stakes in the scene if she loses the argument with Bobby? What will happen if he leaves?

Consider Kathy's pride, fear, and love in this situation with her son.

Questions to Explore for Bobby

Does Bobby really believe Kathy's a bad mom?

As Bobby's sexuality is awakened, so is Kathy's as a single mother. How does that add tension?

Bobby wants discipline and love but he needs a father too. Is he afraid of his father, ashamed, or just tired of his bad behavior?

Questions to Explore for Michael

Why does Michael learn to forgive his mom?

How does the loss of his mouse bring him closer to his mother?

                    KATHY (CONT'D)
          It wasn't pain or hurt or death that
          he saw. And it wasn't the face of a
          murderer.

(Kathy tilts Clare's head up, away from the dirt. Up,
toward...)

CLARE'S POV

(The majesty of the trees. The sun setting again as it did
in the opening.)

(Off the silhouette of the two women standing alone, side by
side, with the redwoods...)

Start Scene ──────────►   DISSOLVE TO:

EXT. WARREN CABIN — NIGHT

(Rick's bike is nowhere in sight as Kathy walks up the dirt
driveway.)

INT. WARREN CABEN — NIGHT

(Kathy enters slowly. A note on the table says simply,
"Michael's asleep. Bobby's in charge till I get back."

Kathy walks to the door of Bobby's room and knocks loudly.)

                    KATHY
          Look, Robert John Warren. You and I
          need to talk.

(He does not respond.)

                    KATHY (CONT'D)
          Fine. I need to talk. To a door.
          To the wall. To my son...
               (deep breath)
          Look, I'm not gonna lie about what
          staying with me will be like. Hard.
          I'm going to expect more out of you
          than anybody ever expected out of
          me. No excuses. No compromises.
               (to herself)
          I compromised my life into this place.
          I don't want to compromise yours.
               (beat, no response)
          So, I guess that's what I had to
          say. Think about it. Fast. No
          more stringing me along. This isn't
          a power play. It's a family. My
          family. And it's going to run by my
          rules — or not at all.
                    (MORE)

                              KATHY (CONT'D)
                         (going boldly where
                         she has not gone
                         before)
                    So I want an answer tonight. Before
                    your father gets back.

        (Bobby opens his door. It's clear he's been crying.)

                              BOBBY
                    He's not coming back tonight. You
                    know that.

                              KATHY
                    I'm not taking that as an excuse to
                    not sleep tonight worrying about
                    what you're gonna do tomorrow. I'm
                    not --

                              BOBBY
                    I'm staying with you.

                              KATHY
                    You... Are?

                              BOBBY
                    At least you say when you made a
                    mistake.

                              KATHY
                    Never one of your father's strong
                    points.

                              BOBBY
                    I only wanted to live with him to
                    make him live up to his obligations.

                              KATHY
                    And you just now figured it wasn't
                    gonna happen?

                              BOBBY
                    I don't remember him ever being nice
                    to you. And somebody should be.
                    Why'd you ever love him in the first
                    place?

                              KATHY
                    Because when he was younger, he was
                    a lot like you.

        Bobby smiles -- for the first time in a long time.

                              KATHY (CONT'D)
                    Do me a favor. Get some sleep.

                        BOBBY
        Do me one?
            (off Kathy's look)
        Get over Dad.

                        KATHY
        I'll try.

(Kathy tousles his hair. Bobby goes back into his room.
Kathy walks down the hall, pausing at,)

THE DOOR TO MICHAEL'S ROOM

(and moving on. Even she can't handle all life's crises in
one night so she turns into her own)

BEDROOM

(strips off her uniform, slips on some waffle-weave sweats
and crawls into bed -- alone. She flips on her radio,
programmed to an oldies station which is right in the middle
of Linda Rondstadt's *Long, Long Time* ("'Cause I've done,
everything I know. To try and make you mine. And I think
I'm gonna love you, for a long, long time.")

Kathy starts to cry from frustration and loneliness and just
plain relief -- as Michael enters in his Air and Space Museum
pajamas and interrupts.)

                        KATHY (CONT'D)
        You okay, honey?

                        MICHAEL
        I was dreaming about my mice... mouse.

                        KATHY
        I'm sorry. I should've been more
        careful with Wilbur.

(She hugs him. He lets her.)

                        MICHAEL
        Least you didn't bash him on purpose.

                        KATHY
        Your Aunt Joanne's just got a
        different way of doing things...

                        MICHAEL
        You think Orville's gonna be okay
        alone?

                        KATHY
        Sure. Now he won't have to worry
        about any pesky sibling rivalry.

(Michael's not completely buying the b.s.)

                              KATHY (CONT'D)
                    Should we have just left them both
                    for the owls? Like Aunt Joanne said?
                    Then you could imagine they were
                    both still alive an digging in some
                    other boy's birdseed.

                              MICHAEL
                         (after a beat)
                    No. I still have Orville. If we'd've
                    left them for the owls, I wouldn't
                    have anything.

                              KATHY
                    Just like if I'd've missed knowing
                    your dad, I wouldn't have you. Or
                    Bobby.

(Michael climbs in to bed and hogs the covers. Kathy doesn't
mind. She switches off the radio, snuggles closer to Michael
and finally closes her eyes.)

EXT. WARREN CABIN — NIGHT

(A mother bear ambles along in the bright moonlight, digging
in the trash containers along the road we saw the school bus
travel in the opening.)

                              KATHY (V.O.)
                    That was the day I learned
                    expectations aren't so bad.

(She brings some tasty tidbit back to her two baby bears who
are trying to hide in the brush.)

                              KATHY (V.O.) (CONT'D)
                    And something else, too...

(One of the young bears ambles out, fumbles with a trash can
lid for a beat...)

                              KATHY (V.O.) (CONT'D)
                    If we don't marry the men of our
                    dreams...

(...And succeeds in popping it off.)

                              KATHY (V.O.) (CONT'D)
                    ...we raise them.

(The mother bear ambles over and nuzzles her cub with pride.)

                                                    FADE OUT

                         THE END

OVERVIEW FOR *NURSES WHO KILL*...WRITTEN BY ANN NOBLE AND CREATED BY ANN NOBLE AND CHANE'T JOHNSON (COPYRIGHT © WGAW 2008)

The title tells you so much. You should be able to glean what you need from the script. Conjure up the mood and tone of the scene as you explore your world. Murder is at the core of the piece, but there can still be moments of levity. Make sure you study the pace and style of webisodes if you are unfamiliar with this kind of Internet entertainment. A short story might be a good frame of reference for this. Once you have done your homework for this scene, keep searching the Internet to find out more about current Web series.

                        NURSES WHO KILL...

INT. AN INTERROGATION ROOM - DAY

PAUL's face--a sweet earnest face--LIGHTS UP from the single
over-head lamp that SOMEONE has just switched on. Paul is at
a table. He is nervous. He squints in the light, at--

TWO FIGURES looming in the darkness, across the room.

                    FIGURE #1
          So, "Paul", what seems to be the
          problem?

                    PAUL
          Uh...well... It's my mother.

                    FIGURE #1
          She's the problem.

                    PAUL
          Yes. Well, yes. Sort of.

                    FIGURE #2
          We don't have time for "sort of".

                    PAUL
          Yes. Yes, I know that. I wouldn't
          have...contacted you if I wasn't
          sure that I...wanted--

                    FIGURE #2
          We don't have time for "wanted".

>   PAUL
>   Do you have any time at all?

Figure #2 growls and makes an aggressive move towards Paul,
who shrinks in his chair, but Figure #1 pulls #2 back.

>   FIGURE #1
>   (to #2)
>   Easy, Spesh.
>   (to Paul)
>   What my colleague meant is--

>   FIGURE #2
>   We don't have time for "want", what
>   we do have time for is "need".

>   PAUL
>   I need this! I do. I really do.

>   FIGURE #1
>   Then you have to say it, Paul.

>   PAUL
>   I need...my mother...dead.

#1 and #2 high five.   Then they step forward, into the light.
They are--

NANCY (#1) and SPECIAL K (#2). Nancy is a tiny white woman,
cool as a cucumber. Special K is a big black woman, hot as a
jalapeno. They are both in pristine 1950s nurse's outfits,
complete with "the hats".

Paul looks between them.

>   PAUL (CONT'D)
>   You're not kidding.

>   NANCY
>   Very rarely, Paul.

Nancy lays a CLIPBOARD with an attached pen on the table.

>   NANCY (CONT'D)
>   We need you to fill out these
>   forms. Initials where the blue
>   sticky-arrows indicate and full
>   signatures at the red ones.

>   PAUL
>   Wait, I don't understand.

>   SPECIAL K
>   What did we say about what we do
>   and do not have time for?!

>   PAUL
>   I'm sorry, I just don't see why you
>   need me to authorize a colonoscopy?

                    SPECIAL K
          Just in case.

                    NANCY
          No!
              (snatching the clipboard)
          These are the wrong forms.

                    PAUL
          Wait, are you guys <u>actually</u> nurses?

                    NANCY
          Exactly what part of our wardrobe
          is unclear to you, Paul?

                    PAUL
          None. Of it.

                    NANCY
          Excellent. I'm Nancy. And this is
          Special K.

                    PAUL
          What's the K stand for?

                    SPECIAL K
          It stands for none of your fu--

THE JAMES BOND THEME PLAYS.

INT. A POSH FLAT - NIGHT

CLOSE ON a SIDEKICK. The James Bond Theme is its RINGTONE
for a text message. THE MANICURED HAND of a young woman with
a fantastic spray tan picks up the device.

                    PAUL (V.O.)
          So my mother is having this party,
          at her house in La Jolla.

The display on the Sidekick reads: WE NEED YOU. N & SP K.

                    PAUL (V.O.) (CONT'D)
          And everyone is going to be there,
          and I mean, everyone.

The Hand quickly texts back. On the display: I'M IN.

EXT. THE LAWN OF A POSH HOUSE IN ORANGE COUNTY - DAY

A PARTY is in swing. A very posh, very boring, very
Republican, VERY post-nine-hole late afternoon soiree. The
men are too tan and the women are too young. Or too old
pretending to be too young.

Everyone has a cocktail. Everyone is quietly trying to
impress...everyone else. Until--

THE MANICURED HAND deftly extracts a full champagne flute
from a tray of flutes dexterously handled by a ridiculously
experienced WAITER.

The flute arrives at the mouth of--

MONROE. She is built. She is beautiful. And she has
planned it that way. She is "somewhere" between 20 and 40.
She's also planned that as well. Today, she is 26 1/2. And
she is...perfect. If Jackie O only had a little sister...

As Monroe wades through the sea of Neo-Cons:

> MONROE
> Excuse me, pardon me. Excuse me.
> Oops, pardon me. Sir.

All eyes follow her as she downs her champagne with one hand
and holds her CHIHUAHUA (in the same outfit) in the other.

She continues to weave amongst the floral linen crowd until--

There she is:

PAULETTE. Her hair is "red". Her make up is a just bit too
much. Her dress is/was perfect in the 80s. But she does
have more money than God, so she is surrounded by an elite
CIRCLE OF FRIENDS. They "listen" as she prattles on and on.

Monroe arrives. With her dog. With a star-struck smile.

> MONROE (CONT'D)
> Oh, my... Are you...Paul's Mama?

> PAULETTE
> (nodding)
> Paulette, yes.

> MONROE
> Oh...my. Well, Paul has just told
> me so much about you.

Paulette is very pleasantly surprised.

EXT. THE "AMBULANCE" (MOVING) - DAY

...is a flawless white 1968 mustang. It speeds along a
street. Special K drives. Nancy "navigates".

> NANCY (V.O.)
> We're going to be late.

> SPECIAL K (V.O.)
> Blame it on these dumb-ass, over-
> medicated uppity women drivers.

> NANCY (V.O.)
> I meant, you're going the wrong
> way.

```
                    SPECIAL K (V.O.)
          I'm going towards the ocean.

                    NANCY (V.O.)
          The Pacific or the Atlantic?

                    SPECIAL K (V.O.)
          Where's the sun?

                    NANCY (V.O.)
          Where it always is.

                    SPECIAL K (V.O.)
          Aw....

     The Ambulance does a U-Turn.

                    SPECIAL K (V.O.) (CONT'D)
          ...mother fu--
```

Questions to Explore for Paul

What did Paul's mother do that made him want to murder her?

He comes from a wealthy family. Is this only about money?

What will Paul gain from killing his mother?

Questions to Explore for Nancy

Think of a very strong inner monologue for Nancy, since she's so calm on the outside.

Figure out what the history is between Nancy and Special K.

What led Nancy to love to kill? Did her nursing profession drive her to murder?

What are three trigger events that have made her murder people?

Questions to Explore for Special K

She seems to be free and open with her smart comments, but what are her insecurities?

What pain does killing people alleviate for Special K?

Who would Special K secretly want to be?

Questions to Explore for Monroe

Monroe could have anything with her looks and charm, so why does she agree to do this?

Why is Monroe attracted to dangerous situations?

Questions to Explore for Paulette

Dig deeper behind the façade of a superficial wealthy lifestyle and find Paulette's vulnerabilities and insecurities.

What has Paulette done to provoke her son's actions?

OVERVIEW FOR *SMUDGE* WRITTEN BY RACHEL AXLER

The play opens with Nick and Colby, a typical couple in their late twenties, expecting a newborn. They are nervously anticipating parenthood, but their hopes for the future are dashed when Colby gives birth to a little abnormal girl she nicknames Smudge. The monologue takes place after the birth as Colby is grappling with the truth about her baby.

SMUDGE

Scene Two

(**COLBY** *in a hospital gown. No longer pregnant. She talks to the audience.*)

COLBY. I think I thought it would be bigger.

They hand it to Nick immediately, like they can't wait to get rid of it. Like they think I'd hurt it. Like, "Take a look at the rest of your life," and I'm like: this is a mistake. Right?

It's sort of purplish-grey. And it's skinny, so skinny, except for its head, which is immeasurably huge. I laugh. It's all a big joke.

"Take this mangled mass," I say. "This tired, poor, mangled mass."

"Give me my tiny form," I say. "Where is it? My perfect tiny form."

The nurses won't look me in the eye. They cast concerned glances toward my chin. They whisper. Watch the corners of my mouth for clues. The doctor comes in, three brisk strides. Tells us they need it back now. He talks to a space near my shoulder.

They wash it, dry it off. It's a quiet thing. It whispers. I count one head. Shading for a torso. A sort of nub. A sort of spike. A point, like a tail, or like a talon, near the bottom. Sort of like a jellyfish. Sort of like something that's been erased. The doctor rushes it away and puts it under a glass, to serve for dinner.

This is how I see it. Under glass, covered in tubes and tape. The eye has opened. Coils of fur grow on it, in odd places.

And my husband loves it.

Originally produced in New York City in 2010 by
Women's Project
Julie Crosby, Producing Artistic Director

SCENE CONSIDERATIONS FOR *SMUDGE*

As the play unfolds, the couple faces their fears with frank talk about their freakish child. This is a dark comedy, but remember feelings of love, horror, and sorrow lie at the core of this painful life experience. We only laugh because the situation is so dire, and we must get relief from the angst we experience.

Rachel Axler's critically acclaimed play challenges traditional beliefs in this monologue. Don't be tempted to go outside the realm of reality with this piece. Consider what it would be like to be the parent of a deformed child. Understand the real-life challenges and feelings of guilt, shame, adoration, and disappointment. Motherhood is supposed to be idyllic, but reality challenges this every day for Colby.

Prepare and rehearse your monologue with all the clues that you are given in this book, and if possible, record your performance. If you want to enrich your learning experience, read the entire play and revisit your work. Record the soliloquy again. Analyze each version and note how you can improve your acting choices in the future when you only have an isolated monologue.

Questions to Explore for Colby

What did she hope her child would be?
How does she shield herself from the truth?
Does she feel like a failure as a mother?
What feelings of love does Colby have for Smudge?
How do the tubes add to Colby's alienation?
Why is she so jealous of Nick's relationship with the baby?
Do hormones play a role in her state?
Is Colby in shock?
Can Colby be her own harshest critic?
How does talking about the grotesque nature of the child help
    Colby cope?

Appendix I: General Script Analysis Checklist

◗ Name, occupation, and age
◗ Marital status
◗ Important family or friends in your life

QUESTIONS TO CONSIDER

- Who are you? What are you doing? Where are you?
- What is the story about?
- What do you plan to do right after the scene?
- What is your last line?
- What is your first line?
- Where are you specifically? (What location, building, or room? Does it have sentimental value to you?)
- What are all of your senses feeling right before you begin the scene?
- Define three significant objects in your space.
- What happened one minute, one day, and one year prior to the scene?
- What are you fighting for?
- What is your scene partner fighting for?
- Is your partner a stranger, lover, friend, family member, or foe?
- What is the most unexpected thing that is said or that you say or discover?

- When and where was the last time you made love (if applicable)?
- How are you and your scene partner changed after the scene?

BACKGROUND CHECK

✓ What are you hiding from your scene partner?

✓ What new information is revealed?

✓ What psychological buttons does your scene partner or your situation push?

✓ What diverts you from your objective?

✓ What is your physical level of comfort? Are you hot, cold, hungry, drunk, or hurt?

✓ What time of day is it?

✓ What is new and old in the scene from your life?

✓ How long have you wanted to say this?

✓ Will anyone be hurt by your actions?

✓ What is your social status, and how will it change in the scene?

✓ Who is the most important figure in your life?

✓ Who hurt you and loved you when you were a child?

✓ Are you repressing or expressing feelings?

✓ Imagine you are looking through your family album and see all the significant events.

✓ How many places have you lived in your life?

Appendix II: Acting Resource Internet Links

*Please note: Websites can change, check for key words and use them if the sites don't work. Be aware of pop-up ads on free sites.

- **Acting Job Listings**
  Key words: Acting Jobs
  - *www.entertainmentcareers.net*
  - *www.backstage.com/bso/index.jsp*
- **Acting Unions**
  Key words: Acting Unions
  SAG
  - *www.sag.org*
  AFTRA
  - *www.aftra.org*
  Equity
  - *www.actorsequity.org*
- **Award-Winning Characters**
  Key words: Acting Oscars
  - *www.filmsite.org*
- **Characters**
  Key words: Character Archetypes
  Wikipedia Archetypes
  - *http://en.wikipedia.org/wiki/Archetype#Jungian_archetypes*

Archetypical Characters TV
- *http://tvtropes.org/pmwiki/pmwiki.php/Main/ArchetypalCharacter*

Character Archetypes
- *www.listology.com/list/character-archetypes*

● **Classic Movies and TV**

Key words: Classic Movies and Television

AMC
- *www.amctv.com*

Turner Classic
- *www.tcm.com*

AFI
- *www.afi.com*

The Classic TV Database
- *http://classic-tv.com*

● **Dialects**

Key words: International Dialects of English Archive
- *http://web.ku.edu/~idea/*

● **Genres**

Key words: Genres film, television, and theater
- *www.imdb.com/Sections/Genres/*

● **Headshot Sites**

Ray Bengston
- *www.eyekool.com*

● **History**

Key word: History
- *www.history.com*

● **Monologues**

Key words: Free Monologues

Free Auditions for Monologues and Study
- *http://auditionpreparation.com*

Horton's StagePage.info

- *www.stagepage.info/monologs/wintermono.html#locoparentis*

Monologue Archive

- *www.monologuearchive.com*

- **Movement**

Key words: Acting Movement Techniques

Actors Movement Studio

- *www.actorsmovementstudio.com*

Alexander Technique Instruction

- *www.alexandertechworks.com*

- **Movie List Databases**

Key words: Movie Databases

The Internet Movie Database

- *www.imdb.com*

- **Online Audition and Casting Sites**

Key words: Actors Auditions Online

Actors Access

- *www.actorsaccess.com*

Casting About

- *https://www.castingabout.com*

LA Casting

- *www.lacasting.com/la_home.asp*

- **Professional Resident Theaters**

Key words: Lort Theatres

League of Resident Theatres

- *http://lort.org*

- **Sides Online**

Key words: TV audition sides

Showfax.com

- *www.showfax.com*

- **Tongue Twisters**
  Key words: Tongue Twisters
    - *www.uebersetzung.at/twister/en.htm*
- **Visual Resources**
  Key words: Visual References Online
  Google
    - *www.google.com*
  Yahoo
    - *www.yahoo.com*
  Key words: Popular Culture and Current Media References,
  Broadcast Yourself
  YouTube
    - *www.youtube.com*
- **Web and Independent Series Awards**
  Key words: Webisode Awards
  The Streamy Awards
    - *http://streamys.org*
  The Webby Awards
    - *www.webbyawards.com*

Appendix III:
Professionalism Checklist

- I have my marketing tools up to date.
- I have everything ready for a last-minute audition.
- I am reachable and return phone calls.
- I'm prompt and reliable.
- I constantly work on parts and I can learn lines as needed.
- I am a team player and take direction well.
- I bring my audition roles to a performance level.
- I take care of my health.
- I don't bad-mouth my agent when I'm not going out on auditions.
- I am fit.
- My wardrobe is ready and organized.
- I network and market my skills on my own.
- I take classes and/or perform regularly.
- I research agents and casting directors before sending materials.

Appendix IV: Tips for Selecting Monologues

▶ Don't wait until an audition; make sure you have different monologues ready for a variety of situations.

▶ Review monologues from classes or scan the Internet regularly and save material that is right for you to work on in the future.

▶ Use a good resource guide to get a broad understanding of material that might be right for you.

▶ Only write monologues for yourself if you can create credible scripts.

▶ Try to avoid overexposed pieces and monologues tied to a particular star.

▶ Study material in the arenas in which you will be auditioning for parts.

▶ If you want to do theater, study classical and current plays and monologues. Find regional and new playwrights to avoid clichéd roles.

▶ Use compilation books for film and TV scripts to find ideas for material, download current sides from casting sites, and seek roles from independent writers and lesser-known authors.

▶ If you do TV commercials, practice ads from casting Websites and magazines or transcribe spots to practice.

▶ Seek a second eye to evaluate your choices. If you can't afford a coach, build an acting network to work on monologues as well as scenes for auditions.

▶ Always seek other materials such as books, stories, and real-life testimonials in magazines to tailor for auditions if you or a talented writer can rewrite the material. Just keep any copyright infringements in mind too.

▶ Select age-appropriate monologues.

Appendix V: Character Type Checklist

Check off and explore what might apply to you:

TYPES	COMMERCIAL	TV EPISODE	FILM
Age Ranges/Types			
Parent	☐	☐	☐
Teen	☐	☐	☐
Grandparent	☐	☐	☐
Spouse	☐	☐	☐
General Roles			
Hero	☐	☐	☐
Heroine	☐	☐	☐
Villain	☐	☐	☐
Compulsive Neurotic	☐	☐	☐
Quirky	☐	☐	☐
Intellectual	☐	☐	☐
Techie	☐	☐	☐
Druggie	☐	☐	☐
Mystic	☐	☐	☐
Criminal	☐	☐	☐
Cop	☐	☐	☐

TYPES	COMMERCIAL	TV EPISODE	FILM
Victim	☐	☐	☐
Psychopath	☐	☐	☐
Healer	☐	☐	☐
Alcoholic	☐	☐	☐
The Innocent	☐	☐	☐
Upper-class Snob	☐	☐	☐
Lower Class	☐	☐	☐
Working Class	☐	☐	☐
Student	☐	☐	☐
Athlete	☐	☐	☐
Bitch	☐	☐	☐
Bully	☐	☐	☐
Singer	☐	☐	☐
Dancer	☐	☐	☐
Model	☐	☐	☐
Do-gooder	☐	☐	☐

General Professional Fields to Consider for Roles

	COMMERCIAL	TV EPISODE	FILM
Legal	☐	☐	☐
Medical	☐	☐	☐
Private Investigation	☐	☐	☐
Law Officer	☐	☐	☐
Government	☐	☐	☐
Intelligence	☐	☐	☐
Education	☐	☐	☐
Aviation	☐	☐	☐
Military	☐	☐	☐
Business	☐	☐	☐
Food Industry	☐	☐	☐

TYPES	COMMERCIAL	TV EPISODE	FILM
Politics	☐	☐	☐
Agriculture	☐	☐	☐
High Tech	☐	☐	☐
Organized Crime	☐	☐	☐
Beauty/Fashion	☐	☐	☐
Entertainment	☐	☐	☐
Artist	☐	☐	☐

Commercial Products That Are Right for Your Type

	COMMERCIAL	TV EPISODE	FILM
Dental	☐	☐	☐
Hair	☐	☐	☐
Perfume	☐	☐	☐
Cologne	☐	☐	☐
Food	☐	☐	☐
Cars	☐	☐	☐
Clothes	☐	☐	☐
Computers	☐	☐	☐
Games	☐	☐	☐
Office Products	☐	☐	☐
Junk Food	☐	☐	☐
Pet Products	☐	☐	☐
Finance	☐	☐	☐
Credit Cards	☐	☐	☐
Pharmaceuticals	☐	☐	☐
Home Repair	☐	☐	☐
Phones	☐	☐	☐
Children's Products	☐	☐	☐
Fitness/Sports	☐	☐	☐
Household products	☐	☐	☐

TYPES	COMMERCIAL	TV EPISODE	FILM
Jewelry	☐	☐	☐
Investment Firms	☐	☐	☐
Health	☐	☐	☐
Appliances	☐	☐	☐
Department Stores	☐	☐	☐
Discount Stores	☐	☐	☐

Appendix VI: Tongue Twisters

*Please make sure to warm up and stretch your tongue before and after doing any vocal work.

Tupelo tree, dip me low once, not twice, but don't drop me tonight!

Ask for caps of colors green because coral can get cowboys mean, Madge.

Cap the gap and be gone, don't dawdle by the dark tiny town square, scram Sam.

Silly shy Sarah sings something sassy silently since she's been taciturn too long.

Cads can't cook cauliflower and corn especially for great big greenhorns, so be gone!

At bat, he made a mad tap, perhaps he'll head home if it goes crack. Can you hear that?

I took the big brown book; can't you tell, Dale?

Good cans cook with hardwood wood burning bright below the branch.

Tell the deli owner no new news can come to hungry eaters of spoiled ham!

Operator oh ow ah, you've got great vocal chords, what are the odds?

Dan, do you tan with a fierce flame or fling fire at your nose?

Send me something shiny so I can sing and sashay at the badlands ball.

Gads, could cads and goons have gone wild Wilfred, why?

Tipsily, Dirk fell down the dark dip in the driveway to a toothy tune.

Ah ha ha! Oh ho ho ha! Here's my highfalutin hat. How grand can a great man stand?

Bring the bad book here, Bobby, before I break the bank buying another naughty best seller.

Stop pop, the poor pauper needs a penny. Please pass it over.

Toddle, doodle, diddle, tee-he, what a silly song sang Herbert ha-ha!

Wow will we win the wily wager willingly, Wilbur?

Humpty had a lump he couldn't get shrunk and that stunk so he sunk.

Okay, Kaye, can we spill good grape wine one more time before we dine?

Spill a bit of birdseed so she shall sing a shameful song.

Oh, ho, ho, ho, ha, ha, ha! Droll trolls laugh longingly like me.

Wring a round of laundry Lucy so we can play a lute lightly at the longshoremen's ball.

Lemon-lime is so sublime for lots of lost sailors shivering in the long snake-like line.

Abacus, abacus, can you make my cold hard cash come back again as glimmering gold?

Ears of eel's leak oil all the time so don't rush or you'll end up in so much slush!

Oink-oink, all the pink pork is fat foul food and undercooked good fellow, so flee fast or fight for your life!

Purple pebbles pick up light in pools laden with petite pink petals.

Do you too dance in the light of the maroon moon on a monsoon?

Mother, Mary may marry me tomorrow maybe if I make a million in the mine.

Fancy father's response to that rash remark, rather odd for an ocelot's sole son don't you think?

Pick the portly pig upright and row rightly to the left along the round river, Roger.

Time a dime could give a dim sum supper special on Saturdays sometimes, Shelly; shall we sample such a sumptuous fare?

Vermouth very, *very* velvety Vera, will you please pass it politely perchance?

Smooth Sherry will wait for a later date, time to dine to a dangerous tune, Dora!

Late maid, late maid, clean counter clockwise on the counter and catch up, chop-chop or you'll miss a messy spot!

Tall dark tan Dan had a flimsy filmy fan for the first day of fall for Florence.

Herbert took a quick look at the catch he caught and threw the frightful fish far back quietly so it should not splash.

Look crook, the stack is sitting in the back so get a grip before it falls fast or you'll be caught aghast.

Unctuous dogs dream deliriously of tipping lots of sharp logs afloat to dislodge dubious dwellers holding a host of haughty hogs.

Ask a time-consuming task to be done with a ton of toil under the sun and you're sure to boil and spoil Shelly so stop being such a silly selfish girl.

He-haw, ha, ha, hailed the horrific hog mocking the mischievous donkey dancing daintily on the dazzling dune.

Why would white woolen sox carry a scary fox farther, father figure that!

Tad, does Dad do tongue twisters in his bed because he can't get good leverage of his lingual muscle without a sublime silent slumber so straight ahead?

Tom may marry a mild-mannered tart because she is so smart and not such a brassy babe.

Egads, I'm glad you can catch your larcenous lies, little lightweight funny flippant fly!

Puppies pump tails fast to get past pesky purple pachyderms pondering the impropriety of policemen's improper parking tickets.

Rah, rah, rah, Roger, reindeer run rapidly with ribbons tethered to their tails. I'm right!

Suggested Readings

Adler, Stella. *The Technique of Acting.* New York: Bantam Books, 1990.

Axler, Rachel. *Smudge.* New York: Samuel French Inc., 2010.

Beard, Jocelyn A., ed. *Monologues from Classic Plays: 468 B.C. to 1960 A.D.* Newbury, VT: Smith and Kraus, 1993.

Caine, Michael. *Acting in Film: An Actor's Take on Movie Making.* Edited by Maria Aitken. Revised Expanded Edition. New York: Applause Books, 2000.

Cameron, Julia. *The Artist's Way: A Spiritual Path to Higher Creativity.* 10th Anniversary Edition. New York: Jeremy P. Tarcher/ Putnam, 2002.

Carnegie, Dale. *How To Win Friends & Influence People.* Reissue Edition. New York: Simon & Schuster, 2009.

Chubbuck, Ivana. *The Power of the Actor: The Chubbuck Technique.* New York: Gotham, 2004.

Grun, Bernard and Eva Simpson. *The Timetables of History: A Horizontal Linkage of People and Events.* New York: Simon & Schuster, 2005.

Hagen, Uta, with Haskel Frankel. *Respect for Acting.* Second Edition. Hoboken, NJ: John Wiley & Sons, 2008.

Hooks, Ed. *The Audition Book: Winning Strategies for Breaking into Theater, Film and Television.* Third Edition. New York: Back Stage Books, 2000.

———. *The Ultimate Scene and Monologue Sourcebook, Updated and Expanded Edition: An Actor's Reference to Over 1,000 Scenes and*

Monologues from More than 300 Contemporary Plays. Second Edition. New York: Back Stage Books, 2007.

Karshner, Roger. *You Said a Mouthful: Tongue Twisters to Tangle, Titillate, Test and Tease.* Toluca Lake, CA: Dramaline Publications, 1993.

Kostroff, Michael. *Letters from Backstage: The Adventures of a Touring Stage Actor.* New York: Allworth Press, 2005.

Manderino, Ned. *All About Method Acting.* Los Angeles: Manderino Books, 1985.

Meisner, Sanford, and Dennis Longwell. *Sanford Meisner on Acting.* New York: Vintage Books, 1987.

Nicholas, Angela. *99 Film Scenes for Actors.* New York: Avon Books, 1999.

Olivier, Laurence. *Confessions of an Actor: An Autobiography.* New York: Simon & Schuster, 1985.

Schulman, Michael, and Eva Mekler. *The Actor's Scenebook: Scenes and Monologues from Contemporary Plays.* New York: Bantam Books, 1984.

Shurtleff, Michael. *Audition: Everything an Actor Needs to Know to Get the Part.* New York: Walker & Company, 2003.

Simon, Neil. *Neil Simon Monologues: Speeches from the Works of America's Foremost Playwright.* Acting Edition. Edited by Roger Karshner. Rancho Mirage, CA: Dramaline Publications, 1996.

Smith, Marisa and Kristin Graham, editors. *Monologues from Literature: A Sourcebook for Actors.* New York: Fawcett Columbine, 1990.

Smith, Marisa, and Amy Schewel, editors. *The Actor's Book of Movie Monologues.* New York: Penguin Books, 1986.

Spolin, Viola. *Improvisation for the Theater: A Handbook of Teaching and Directing Techniques (Drama and Performance Studies).* Third Edition. Evanston, IL: Northwestern Univ. Press, 1999.

Stanislavski, Constantin. *An Actor Prepares.* New York: Routledge, 1989.

Strasberg, Lee. *A Dream of Passion: The Development of the Method*. Edited by Evangeline Morphos. New York: Plume, 1988.

Truby, John. *The Anatomy of Story: 22 Steps to Becoming a Master Storyteller*. New York: Faber & Faber, 2008.

Warhit, Doug. *Book the Job: 143 Things Actors Need to Know to Make It Happen*. Los Angeles: Dau Publishing, 2003.

Williams, Tennessee. *The Glass Menagerie*. Reprint Edition. New York: New Directions, 1999.

———. *The Night of the Iguana*. Reprint Edition. New York: New Directions, 2009.

About the CD

The CD begins with brief reminders about everyday auditions. There are tips for warming up and behaving professionally at auditions. Then three industry professionals share stories and advice about how to succeed in the industry. You'll learn firsthand from actors Mark Zimmerman and Lee Garlington how they booked jobs on Broadway, film, and TV. Bob Luke gives a talent manager's perspective on how you can maximize your career potential. Their biographies can be found below.

Mark Zimmerman

Over his thirty-plus years as an actor, Mark has appeared in seven Broadway shows (including *West Side Story*, *A Catered Affair [1999]*, *The Rainmaker*, *On the Twentieth Century*, and *Brigadoon*), the National tours of *Mamma Mia* and *Kiss of the Spider Woman*, and at numerous Off-Broadway and regional theaters. His television credits include *30 Rock*, *Royal Pains*, *Damages*, *Law & Order* (in the recurring role of Judge Nathan Murphy), and *Murphy Brown*. He has appeared in the films *The Thomas Crown Affair*, *A Price Above Rubies*, *Dash and Lilly*, *Claire Dolan*, *The Giraffe*, *For Love or Money*, and *The Bonfire of the Vanities*. He has appeared in over five hundred commercials and has done extensive voice-over and radio work throughout his career. Mark served as president of Actors' Equity Association from 2006 through 2009.

Lee Garlington

Lee Garlington has appeared in more than sixty films, including *Sum of All Fears, Sneakers, Field of Dreams, Cobra, The Babysitter, Lovely and Amazing, Mrs. Harris, Something New, Stick It,* and *Akeelah and the Bee.* Lee has been in thirty Movies-of-the-Week, including *A Killing in a Small Town, Shame, Cold Sassy Tree,* and *The Long Road Home.* She has been a series regular on eleven pilots and six (short-lived) series including *Lenny* and *Townies.* She recurred on *West Wing, Everwood, Southland,* and *Flash Forward.* Currently, she is recurring on *The Whole Truth* and *Friends with Benefits.*

Bob Luke

Top coach and talent manager Bob Luke has a long list of successful clients including award-winning actors. He was the on-set coach for *The Cosby Show,* several New York soap operas, as well as films with Ron Howard, Mel Gibson, Meryl Streep, and Amy Adams, among others.

Bob has discovered and guided many actors to stardom, including Josh Hutcherson *(Journey to the Center of the Earth)*, Matthew Schechter *(Waiting for Godot* on Broadway), John Arthur Greene *(West Side Story* on Broadway), Riley Smith *(24)*, and Sarah Michelle Gellar *(Buffy the Vampire Slayer)*, among others.

Sound Design and Music Composition by Troy Stone

About the Author

I always wanted to be a performer and especially liked singing and dancing. My mother was a natural actor, and she helped me prepare for my role in the high school production of *Harvey*. Then, when I was in college and graduate school, I took production classes. I also acted in productions and was suited for the camera because I wasn't broad or theatrical, and I was good at improvisation.

People told me that I should be an actress, but I didn't pay much attention to these comments because I loved movies and wanted to be a director. Being a teaching assistant to Amos Vogel for his film class at the University of Pennsylvania was a perfect opportunity for me to explore my love of the cinema. I worked in the film and television industry initially, for Emmy®-winning sports producer Bud Greenspan. Learning inspiring stories about great athletes was a wonderful prelude to my acting endeavors.

Eventually, I did get to direct many celebrity promotional segments for HBO. When I first started there, my boss said, "Janet, you have a nice voice, why don't you read this?" That's when I fell in love with doing voice-overs. Subsequently, I studied acting in New York City and worked in film, TV, and theater. Studying improvisation with Paul Sills was invaluable training for the improv show I performed in a comedy club. Meanwhile, I was the voice of Lifetime's Billboards in New York. It was a weekly gig, so that gave me new freedoms as a working mom.

When I moved to Los Angeles, I was fortunate to work and take classes in an entertainment-rich environment. Witnessing my husband win a primetime Emmy® was a wonderful thrill. Doing the voice-over for AMC's star-studded *Nicole Kidman: An American Cinematheque Tribute* was a lot of fun because it combined voice-over and a live performance. In addition, I was the voice of the E! show *Hollywood and Divine: Beauty Secrets Revealed,* and I created twenty-nine character voices for my children's story *Fifi of Fifth Avenue.* I also began to teach voice-over at UCLA Extension and at the SAG Conservatory.

I've learned through the years that acting is about passion, and you can't do it without a desire that drives you to work at it persistently. You may not make a lot of money at first, so it has to be about a love of the craft and the joy of doing it. I hope this book can help you achieve the goals you have set for yourself, and that you will be successful in your pursuits.

Index

body, 15
heart, 15
soul, 15
counterbalance, 19
craft, 25, 58, 81, 113
   practice, 25
create credible roles, 14
creative research, 71
creative spirits, 15
creativity, ix, 3
Criminal Minds, 62
crucial components of tasks, 89
CSI: Crime Scene Investigation, 62
cue lines, ix
Curious Case of Benjamin Button, The,
   45, 79
   Daisy, 45

D
Damon, Matt, 30
   Good Will Hunting, 30
Dancing with the Stars, 20
David, Larry, vii, 48
   Seinfeld, 48
desire, 114
"Desperate," 144
dialogue, 22, 60
   unforeseen circumstances, 60
different styles of acting, 26
   comedies, 26
   commercials, 26
   procedural TV dramas, 26
director, x, 9, 15, 18, 36, 59, 94, 99, 108,
   115
discipline, 113
distinctive traits, 37
"Doctor's Last Call," 146
doubt, 15
drama, 6

E
Earth (Jones), 72
economic factor, 72
elements of script, 47

character description, 47
scene location, 47
time of day, 47
emotional investments, 33
emotional life, 87
emotional triggers, 75
emotionally connected, 14
emotions, 11, 35, 62, 66, 75, 98
   communication of emotions, 11
energy, 14
entertainment business, 118
essential tools, 40
   exercise, 40
   movement classes, 40
establish contact, 116
exercise, 20, 73, 150
   finish the story, 150
   play with situations, 151
   problem solving, 151
   study the play unfolding, 151
exploring roles, 24

F
failure, 5
faith, 15
"Fashion Flair," 140
favorite characters, 56
feedback, 5
Ferreras, Alberto, 163
   My Audition for Almodovar, 163
Ferris Bueller's Day Off, vii, 62
Fey, Tina, 30
   30 Rock, 30
Field of Dreams (Jones), 79
   Costner, Kevin, 79
"First Prize," 142
focus, 25
Ford, Harrison, 55
   Jones, Indiana, 55
"Four O'clock," 131
full plays, x
funds, 113

Books from Allworth Press

Allworth Press is an imprint of Skyhorse Publishing, Inc. Selected titles are listed below.

Voiceovers: Techniques and Tactics for Success
by *Janet Wilcox* (6 × 9, 208 pages, paperback, $24.95)

An Actor's Guide—Making It in New York City, Second Edition
by *Glenn Alterman* (6 × 9, 345 pages, paperback, $24.95)

An Actor's Guide—Your First Year in Hollywood
by *Michael St. Nicholas* (6 × 9, 272 pages, paperback, $19.95)

How To Audition for TV Commercials: From the Ad Agency Point of View
by *W. L. Jenkins* (6 × 9, 208 pages, paperback, $16.95)

Making It on Broadway: Actors' Tales of Climbing to the Top
by *David Wienir* (6 × 9, 288 pages, paperback, $19.95)

The Art of Auditioning: Techniques for Television
by *Rob Decina* (6 × 9, 224 pages, paperback, $19.95)

Creating Your Own Monologue
by *Glenn Alterman* (6 × 9, 256 pages, paperback, $19.95)

An Actor Rehearses: What to Do When and Why
by *David Hlavsa* (6 × 9, 224 pages, paperback, $19.95)

Acting for Film
by *Cathy Haase* (6 × 9, 240 pages, paperback, $21.95)

The Lucid Body: A Guide for the Physical Actor
by *Fay Simpson* (6 × 9, paperback, 224 pages, $19.95)

Actor Training the Laban Way: An Integrated Approach to Voice, Speech, and Movement
by *Barbara Adrian* (7⅜ × 9¼, 208 pages, paperback, $24.95)

Acting the Song: Performance Skills for the Musical Theatre
by *Tracey Moore* (6 × 9, 304 pages, paperback, $24.95)

Clues to Acting Shakespeare, Second Edition
by *Wesley Van Tassel* (6 × 9, 288 pages, paperback, $18.95)

Stage Combat: Fisticuffs, Stunts, and Swordplay for Theater and Film
by *Jenn Boughn* (7¾ × 9⅜, 224 pages, paperback, $19.95)

Digital Technical Theater Simplified: High Tech Lighting, Audio, Video and More on a Low Budget
by *Drew Campbell* (6 × 9, 288 pages, paperback, $24.95)

Building the Successful Theater Company, Second Edition
by *Lisa Mulcahy* (6 × 9, 256 pages, paperback, $24.95)

To see our complete catalog or to order online, please visit *www.allworth.com*.